Dedicated to
Dr. Robert Hutchins
Dr. David Mason
Dr. Robert Swan

There is a tide in the affairs of men when taken at the flood moves on to fortune.

—Shakespeare

These three men in their unique robes of white moved in unison according to God's ticking of the clock of time. They moved on the tide of their God-given wisdom, knowledge, and medical and surgical expertise and turned the ordinary into extraordinary days of fortune.

From the depth of my heart, I thank you for the added years to live, to love, and to enjoy my work of communicating God's love in a culture yearning for meaning.

Our daughter, Jan, and her family, and our son, Ralph, and his family join me to say thank you, and God bless you and your families.

Thank You

We don't walk alone through life, and I wish to express my deep gratitude to the countless friends who walk with me.

When I pull into the gas station, I am reminded to, "Stick to writing. We'll take care of the car."

What a blessing for me to know that cheerful tellers at the bank know how to add—*correctly!* Thank you.

When this "bag lady" comes dragging in her bags of books, the post office crew could groan. But instead, with a smile, they help me to decipher foreign addresses—and remind me to keep writing.

On a rainy day the mailman brought a stack of mail to the door. "Whew," he gasped. "Never saw so much mail." I suggested that he take it home and answer it. With a chuckle he was gone.

When I'm late on Tuesday morning to remember "garbage day," the garbage man waves a greeting and waits while I run down the driveway dragging my garbage container.

Neighbors wave and chat when I take my morning walk and ask about a new book coming out. They also watch my house when I'm gone.

I've almost adopted the young man from U.P.S. who picks up my books so I don't have to drag them to the car for mailing.

Then there's Buddy, the yard man. He's good for a comedy show any day. "I'm here to take care of Ralph's mamma. Yes, sir—Ralph sent me. Can't have no messy yard for his mamma, no, sir. Leaves raked, mowed, and trimmed." We

ALL GOD'S CHILDREN GOT ROBES

MARGARET JENSEN

HARVEST HOUSE PUBLISHERS
Eugene, Oregon 97402

Scripture quotations are from the King James Version of the Bible.

ALL GOD'S CHILDREN GOT ROBES
Copyright © 1996 by Harvest House Publishers
Eugene, Oregon 97402

Cataloging-in-Publication Data

Jensen, Margaret T. (Margaret Tweten), 1916–
    All God's children got robes / Margaret Jensen.
        p.   cm.
    ISBN 1-56507-335-5 (alk. paper)
    1. Jensen, Margaret T. (Margaret Tweten), 1916–   . 2. Christian
biography—United States. 3. Christian life—Anecdotes. I. Title.
BR1725.J43A3   1996   95-34982
209'.2—dc20   CIP
[B]

Printed in the United States of America.

96 97 98 99 00 01 02 / BC / 10 9 8 7 6 5 4 3 2

sit on the swing during a break in the hot day and munch cookies and milk together. *He* should write the stories.

Then my son Ralph sent Diane over to clean "Norwegian." She does! While I'm on the phone making travel plans, she whips through the house and leaves it sparkling. "No way you can do it all," Diane insists. "You need to be in that office and write."

What about my faithful travel agent, Ronda? Since 1984 she has scheduled flights around the world. "Let's try for a later flight. That 7 A.M. is too early." I agree. Thank you!

My beautiful friend Gloria and her husband John work late into the night to run a laundry, dressmaking, and dry-cleaning business. Full of the joy of the Lord, Gloria can tackle anything. "Don't worry, baby, I made big seams. I'll fit that skirt better in the hips. The dress will be ready for the banquet." With a hug and a reminder to, "Take it easy, baby," I'm off to my office.

When my friends across the miles send letters thanking me for the books and urging me to write the next one, I get so excited that I pick up my pen and yellow pad and "just do it"! Thank you for that kind of faith, love, and prayers.

It will never be the same without Harold, my biggest fan, but with a family that reminds me of God's faithfulness I can feel the empty place fill up with their love. You, my friends, know these children and grandchildren through the books: Jan and Jud Carlberg, Heather and Chad; Ralph and Chris Jensen, Shawn, Eric, Sarah, and Kathryn. And when they say, "Grammy, go for it"—I go! Thank you.

Thank you, Les Stobbe, for publishing my first book in 1982 and continuing to encourage me on this journey—eleven books by 1995.

Thank you, Jim Warren, host of "Prime Time America." You're the one with the golden voice who urges me to tell the stories and write.

These are friends of long standing. Then God put new friends to walk with me.

Thank you, Eileen Mason, for introducing me to the Harvest House family. I'm at home in a family of vision and mission.

I'm sure my new editor, Barbara Sherrill, has discovered I write just like I talk—and that has some detours. Thank you for your skill, Barbara, in getting me on the main road.

Harold must chuckle in heaven when he sees Linda Britton praying for the gift of interpretation when she transfers my penciled scrawl to the computer. Her experience as an English tutor helps. Thank you, Linda.

I pray God's blessing on all my family and friends who walk with me. Thank you for keeping me safe with your love and prayers.

MTJ

Contents

The Journey Begins

The Journey Begins

It was January, 1995. I waited in the office and watched Dr. Mason's serious face as he thumbed through a medical folder holding my records.

A warm smile replaced the serious demeanor. "Congratulations. We need to celebrate! Your five-year checkup is great!"

After a brief visit and a big "thank you" hug, I headed for the car.

"Thank You, Lord, for the five years You have given me," I prayed on my way out. "What a gift!"

Inside the car, I shouted out loud and stepped on the gas. Before I knew it, I was going sixty miles per hour in a thirty-five mph zone. The thought of a former ticket took my heavy foot off the gas pedal. I looked for a blue light. Believe me, I usually get caught when I'm doing something wrong.

This time I didn't. I chuckled to myself, "I probably would have given the police officer a hug and smiled all the way to the courthouse."

Nothing could upset me today.

When I returned home, I reached for the telephone and called my daughter Jan, my sisters, my daughter-in-love Chris, my son Ralph, and my eighty-seven-year-old

Uncle Jack and yelled, "I passed!" This was my day, and my report card had all A's.

At the end of the day, when the lights were low and the night was still, I curled up in my husband Harold's leather chair and called to him in heaven. I thanked him for being there when I needed him the most. I'm glad I didn't know he would go home before me, less than two years after I had been diagnosed with cancer.

They were all there in the winter of the soul: my Jan, the breath of springtime, came in the cold of the night; her husband, Jud, ferried her to airports "to be with Mom"; Chris, who came in the blizzard of Christmas Day with a candle and Christmas cup of tea; and Ralph, who plowed through snow and ice in a Jeep to be with Harold and me. Ministers from different denominations joined our beloved pastor emeritus Horace Hilton to pray for me in my storm.

All God's Children Got Robes comes from my journal of the past five years. In the beginning I'm wearing a robe of velvet and lace; all too soon I'm in a "Victoria's Not-So-Secret" see-through hospital gown which covers little. I write of mountains and valleys, fears and doubts, laughter and tears—then the triumph of faith.

Those five years produced three books, a trip to Israel, and thousands of miles across the skies of Canada and America the beautiful.

What a gift from God!

As we journey together through the pages of my journal, cry and laugh with me. When we turn the last page, just shout, "Great is Thy faithfulness, oh Lord, my God!"

Take courage for the road ahead, and remember we don't walk alone. Our times are in God's hands (Psalm 31:15).

Thank you for your love and prayers.

All God's Children Got Robes

1

The Way Home

I *cleared my desk, closed up the office,* and prepared for the annual Christmas banquet at the University of North Carolina in Wilmington.

Harold, my meticulously dressed husband of fifty years (his nickname—"The Kentucky Colonel"), was ready early as usual.

"Margaret," he huffed, "it wouldn't kill you to be early for a change."

"I know, but you'll have to admit that I am never late."

"Margaret, ten minutes to go!" Harold began his ritual countdown.

"I know, Harold."

"Five minutes!"

"Yes, Harold."

Zero! I was ready right on the button and checked myself in the mirror: long black velvet skirt, white lace Victorian blouse, and a cranberry taffeta cummerbund.

Harold fastened the emerald and gold cross around my neck, a gift from a precious friend. He put the mink stole around my shoulders, and I remembered another friend of long ago.

Memories bless us many times.

Harold, the perfectionist, stooped to brush the lint off my suede shoes. Under his approving eye, I was ushered into the car to proceed to the banquet where I was the evening storyteller. Alumni, faculty, and special guests of all or no faiths would be my audience at the University of Carolina. I would face a challenging group of people: younger intellectuals, older traditional Southerners, men and women of power and wealth who shared their expertise to make this university the best.

I had spent the previous weeks in my office pondering and praying for wisdom in approaching this gala evening. Into my heart came the gentle voice, "Tell what you know."

I would!

"I'm taking you back to a long ago time in my early childhood," I began that wintery evening in 1989. "To the people and places of Christmases past..."

My angel mother came from Norway when she was fifteen years old. She worked for a Jewish mistress on Park

Avenue in New York City. This wise Jewish mistress introduced my mother to the library, where she learned the language and culture quickly and became a self-educated woman.

My father came from Norway as a young man to study for the ministry. His dormitory was the furnace room of Chicago University, where he earned his way as the automatic furnace stoker. Books and libraries were his love. Then he met my mother, and they were married in Brooklyn, New York. Later, Papa became the pastor of a small country church in Woodville, Wisconsin. (I had the privilege of speaking at the hundreth anniversary of that white country church and was a guest in the parsonage where I was born.)

On my fifth birthday, we arrived at the Winnipeg, Manitoba, train station. While my parents moved into the parsonage, I decided to "travel" a bit more on my own and landed in the police station to enjoy a birthday party of fish and potatoes. I entertained my new friends with stories from our Norwegian immigrant family. Then we heard the deacon from Papa's new church, "Vell, vell, ve found de little von."

I couldn't understand all the concern. I was having a wonderful time. I knew where I was!

At this time young men were recruited from the Scandinavian countries to work in the "Big Woods," the lumber camps of the Northwest. Immigrants were pouring into the railroad station, and I went with my father to meet the trains. Our home was filled with lonely young immigrants in search of the pot of gold at the end of the rainbow. Sometimes they landed on farms with a bucket under an ornery cow.

Christmas 1923, Mama pulled out all the stops. There would be a traditional Norwegian Christmas dinner for Christmas Eve: lute fisk (a slippery fish we children disliked—but a true Norwegian eats it anyhow), potatoes with melted butter and parsley, vegetables, rice pudding, Jule kakke (Christmas bread), butter cookies, and gallons of coffee. How unlike our usual diet of oatmeal, homemade soup, and wilted vegetables!

Over by the cookstove Papa pulled on his overshoes, buttoned up a heavy coat, and pulled the fur cap over his ears. "Mama, I will go to the railroad station to see if there are lonely men with no place to go."

His footsteps echoed in the snow.

I helped Mama set the long tables. We never knew how many guests we would have, but Mama believed that God could multiply lute fisk and Jule kakke, just as He did the loaves and fish two thousand years ago. It seemed that Mama's meals fed multitudes in her lifetime.

Shouting, laughter, and footsteps in the snow announced the arrival of twenty men from the railroad station. In spite of the crowd, a holy hush descended over the parsonage while Papa asked a Norwegian blessing.

Suddenly, we heard stomping feet on the porch and two men fell in the door—almost frostbitten. They were helped to the table and filled with hot coffee.

Bjorne and John had been in the Big Woods. The barracks were cold, and the diet consisted of oatmeal and salt pork.

"If we stay here we will die," Bjorne had stated simply.

"Ja, that is true," John agreed. "Many have tuberculosis and there is no pay for months. But if we leave we will die."

"Ja, but if we can make it to Pastor Tweten for Christmas Eve, we will make it in this new country."

"So, how do we die? Do we stay and die—or do we die trying?"

So it came to pass that John and Bjorne walked eighty miles in a Canadian winter; hot tea and biscuits were offered in shelters along the way.

That memorable Christmas of 1923 we put the tree in the center of the parlor and decorated it with small candles. We joined hands and danced around the tree singing carols in Norwegian. The instruments were tuned up, Papa played the piano, and the sound of music filled the Canadian winter...

My audience at the University of Carolina seemed to reach out to me to tell more. Somehow I knew the memories of long ago had touched the sophisticated culture before me. Perhaps we shared the same longing for a simpler time when families were close and homes were open to strangers.

"Five years later," I continued, "my father moved us into a small, four-room house—only five-hundred square feet—in Saskatoon, Saskatchewan. We had an outhouse at the end of the path and a water tank in the kitchen. From Mama's rocking chair by the cookstove, we learned life's valuable lessons..."

It was another Christmas Eve in a small house in a strange place. Papa was away on a missionary journey, traveling the roads of Saskatchewan, holding services in schoolhouses. We put up a small tree in the corner of the parlor and made paper ornaments. We always had one present under the tree and a stocking with a whole orange, apple, nuts, and candy. This year, though, there were no presents under the tree. The corner was bare.

And there was no Christmas food!

Mama bustled about, setting the table with her linen tablecloth and fine china.

"Has God forgotten us?" one of my sisters asked.

"Oh, no," Mama hastily replied. "God does not forget his children."

She kept singing Christmas carols.

"Come," Mama finally announced, "into the tub! We get ready for Christmas Eve."

Though Saturday night was bath night, on Christmas Eve we got scrubbed and poured into long underwear regardless.

Mama dressed up for the occasion and gathered her five children around the rocking chair and told the Christmas story: "For God so loved the world, He gave His Son."

Then we sang carols. Then we knew we should be opening gifts.

"But Mama, we have no presents!" we children protested.

"Ja, it is true," Mama nodded her head. "But we have the Gift. So who needs presents? And we won't be hungry when we have oatmeal and even a sugar lump to dip in the coffee."

Suddenly, we heard the sound of stomping feet in the snow. When Mama opened the door, Dr. Ward, pastor of the First Baptist Church of Saskatoon, came in with his young people.

"It came to our attention," Dr. Ward smiled, "that the missionary to the Norwegian settlers had not returned, and we knew how you celebrate Christmas Eve."

The young people came in carrying prepared food to place on the table that was already set! Then fruits, candy, and gifts were placed under the lonely tree in the corner. Pastor Ward read the Christmas story (which we didn't mind hearing again), and we all joined in singing carols.

Before leaving, Dr. Ward extended an invitation for us to attend their traditional Christmas Day dinner. I whispered to my sister Grace, "We are going to be company." We always had people filling our home, but now we were to be honored guests.

As the last of the visitors left, Mama put on the coffeepot. Then we heard another sound—Papa was home!

"Ja, I was lost in a blizzard," Papa shook the snow from his hat and coat, "and I said, 'God, I am lost, but You are not. Lead me to a place of safety so I can get home for Christmas Eve.'"

"What happened, Papa?"

"Ja—a warm presence drew near, and I followed the presence to a shack submerged under the snow. There I met a farmer who I helped to shovel a path to the barn. We milked the cow and gathered eggs and survived the blizzard." He looked at us all. "Now I am home! Look at all the food—and presents!"

"Mama set the table before there was any food," one of my sisters reported.

"Now we thank God for His provision and protection," Papa added.

What a Christmas Eve...

On the way home from the Christmas banquet that evening, Harold remarked about the warm reception to the stories. The comments I had received had been most affirming: "I felt lost in a blizzard of circumstances—but my faith has been renewed."

The evening was over! I put away the mink stole—a far cry from my feedsack dresses in days gone by. The velvet skirt was placed in a bag, and the white lace blouse was ready for another "storytime."

I thought of my friends with their gifts of love—and Harold who bent down to brush the lint from my shoes. He was always ready early.

What I didn't know was that my own journey through a "blizzard"—the dark winter of the soul—was coming soon. Too soon, too soon!

2

All God's Children Got Robes

December 21, 1989—6 A.M.

The world outside is dark and cold. The wind is blowing against the bay window in the breakfast room. I turn up the heat and put the coffee pot on. Harold, my husband of fifty years, is asleep. He will have coffee.

No coffee for me this morning. Today I go to the hospital! Nothing to drink after midnight.

I look around my breakfast room. The Christmas candle on the Scandinavian tablecloth casts a soft glow. The Christmas ornaments on the bay window hold a silent vigil. Camels from Israel, made out of olive wood, march in single file. The baby Jesus sleeps in a tiny manger filled with pine straw.

The wind keeps blowing outside. There's a storm coming.

Just yesterday Christmas joy filled my house. I was baking Jule kakke and Christmas cookies while my list of "honey do's" was checked over twice.

About 350 Christmas letters, with a picture of Harold and me in a sled, had been tucked into envelopes. Harold had gone to the post office to mail them. One last package was to be sent to our daughter Janice—three loaves of Jule kakke for the Carlbergs' Christmas morning. I would finish baking them this very day.

I lined up the other five loaves of the Norwegian treat to be delivered to my neighbors. My granddaughter Kathryn and I could do that later.

Cookies filled colorful tins while music filled the house and my heart.

It was Christmas—the happiest time of the year.

The ring of the telephone shattered the sound of music, and I reached for the phone with flour-smudged hands.

"This is Dr. Mason," the voice on the other end spoke directly. "I'm sorry to give you this report over the telephone, but I scheduled you for surgery on Friday, December 22. Dr. Swann, a skilled oncologist, is your surgeon. The biopsy is positive."

Cancer!

The gynecologist paused uncertainly. He was young—and it was Christmas.

"I have traveled all over this country," I said to him, "and told one message—the faithfulness of God and His great love for us."

It was quiet on the other end.

"I have had seventy-three years of excellent health," I continued, "fifty years married to the same man (however, I did change him—ha!), three children, and six grandchildren. The same God who has been with me all these years won't fail me now."

Then it was over! I held the phone, smeared with flour, and sobbed out my grief. Cancer of the uterus. Tears fell into the dishwater. With the reflexes of my Scandinavian heritage, I immediately cleaned the stove and refrigerator.

"Keep your house in dying-clean condition" came back to me as I scrubbed.

When I was nursing at Cone Hospital in Greensboro, I remembered how the private duty nurses sat at one table and told stories. One elderly nurse told how she had been nursing one patient after another during a flu epidemic years ago. Each night she managed to wash her uniform and polish her shoes, then crawled into bed too exhausted to do any housework.

One day she came home shaking with chills and fever. She had the flu—and no one to take care of her! She looked at the garbage overflowing the can, the dishes in the sink, the laundry piled up, and she knew she would die.

"I won't let the women of First Church come into my house and find this disaster," she told herself.

With superhuman strength she emptied the sink of dishes, put a load of wash in the washer, scrubbed the bathroom and the kitchen floors, and took out the garbage. She put her best sheets and hand-embroidered pillowcases on the bed. After a bath she braided her hair and put on a new nightgown—saved for "in case of an emergency."

She looked at her clean house, crawled into bed, and folded her hands across her chest. "Now—let the ladies of First Church come. Lord, lead me gently home."

When morning came, the sun was streaming in the window. She was in the same position—hands folded across her chest—but drenched in perspiration. Alive!

"Girls, let that be a lesson to you," the old nurse told us. "Keep your house in 'dying-clean condition.'"

So that's what I was doing now. Keeping my house in dying-clean condition. I scrubbed furiously.

I remembered when I was fourteen years old and all my life was mixed up. The boy I liked happened to like my girlfriend. She, in turn, liked someone else.

"Oh, Mama," I cried, "life is so mixed up I could die."

"Ja, ja," Mama answered while she pulled the ironing basket from under the table, "while you are dying—iron!"

Harold returned from the post office and reached for the "honey do" list.

"Sit down, Harold. You won't need the list."

We held each other and wept. The bread for our daughter Jan was baking in the oven, and the aroma of cardamon filled the kitchen.

Harold read Psalm 34, "I will bless the Lord at all times: his praise shall continually be in my mouth."

We prayed together. The tears wouldn't stop, but deep inside I felt a steady beat: "The joy of the Lord is my strength" (Nehemiah 8:10).

"Harold, what about the children?" I worried.

"We have to call the children," he calmly replied.

"Oh, if only we could spare them—and Christmas at that!"

After calling Ralph, our son who lived in Wilmington, Harold dialed Massachusetts to tell our daughter Janice and her husband Jud.

From North Carolina to Florida and Arkansas, the message was relayed to my four sisters, who knew how to march boldly to the throne of grace to find strength and mercy. I called them the "Royal Guard," as we five Tweten sisters stood as one in joy and sorrow.

The final phone call made, I remembered just in time to pull the last loaf of Jule kakke from the oven. There they were—three beautiful loaves for Jan.

Suddenly, the door burst open!

"Mama, Mama." There was Ralph, our youngest—all six foot six and two hundred pounds of him—crying like a child. I was swallowed up in arms of love. Then he prayed, "Oh, God, this is Your child and the enemy won't win. Out of all this, You will work good and bring glory to Your name."

"Come," urged Harold, "let's go to Swensons for lunch."

Our grandsons Shawn, seventeen, and Eric, fourteen, met us, and we were able to calm their fear-filled hearts over milkshakes and hamburgers.

How many times we found ourselves in our favorite corner by the window! Sometimes it was just Harold and me, enjoying a bowl of soup and a sandwich—and on a very hard day, a caramel sundae. Other times Harold took the grandchildren—especially when Katie rolled her eyes. "Papa, were you thinking about Swensons?"

He suddenly thought of Swensons.

I remember when Katie was a little girl, and we were having a particularly heavy storm—thunder rolling, lightning flashing, the works.

"Whew!" Harold came in the door. "What a storm! I'm drenched!"

"Papa," Katie said sweetly, "the power is off here, but I'm sure Swensons has hot coffee."

"Why, Katie. What a great idea!"

She beamed!

"I'm not going out in this storm!" I scowled. "Never!"

"Oh, come on," Harold countered, "get your rain-coat. How can you pass up hot coffee at Swensons?"

Katie, Harold, and I were all alone in Swensons that afternoon—to the delight of our friend, the owner. The storm raged outside, but we had laughter and coffee in-side.

Now we were back at Swensons—and facing a different storm. The thunder and lightning raged on the in-side, but we laughed and talked about the good times anyway. When Ralph and the boys returned to work, faith slipped in through the fears and won!

On our way home from Swensons, I turned to my husband. "Harold, I need a new robe and some gowns and slippers. All God's children got robes," I reminded him. He smiled.

My old familiar robe, worn and frayed, had faced many winter mornings putting on the coffeepot. It was the old wraparound style with ties, and my slippers were fleece-lined—not fit for a fashion show, believe me.

Harold and I rummaged around in the lingerie depart-ment at Belks and bumped into Tennie and Horace Hilton in the underwear department.

We told Horace, our beloved pastor emeritus, about the news... and the need for a decent robe. We invited them over that evening for a time of prayer with our three young pastors—Steve, Jim, and Scott.

We returned home to the practical tasks at hand, beginning with my hallowed place—my office. My desk had to be cleared and my files put in order. My unfinished manuscript cried for attention. I looked at the title, *Prop Up the Leaning Side.* I had never dreamed the day would come when I would need the "propping up."

"Unto Thee, oh, Lord, do I lift up my soul," I prayed as I sorted notes and papers. "Don't let the enemy of doubt and confusion rob me of peace. Direct my thoughts to Thee, my faithful guide through all these years."

I closed my office door when I had finished. It seemed so final.

When the ministers arrived that evening, I had punch and cookies ready for a party.

"This is some way to get you all together," I let them know, "so here we are."

Serious Scott: "But we came to pray."

"I know, but I might as well enjoy a party and prayer together."

Horace, Tennie, Steve, Jim, Scott, Harold, and I gathered in the living room. The tree was decorated. Wrapped gifts were placed carefully under it. Christmas cardamon filled the air with the aroma and joy of Christmas.

Through the night, others came: Father Waters, Peter Stam, Homer, family and friends. They came to pray.

God answers prayer!

Around 10 P.M., the last of the cars pulled out of the driveway, and Harold and I were alone. The bread was waiting to be mailed to Jan. The stove and refrigerator were clean. My bags were packed.

We turned out the lights, and I curled up in Harold's arm. Peace covered us with a blanket of God's grace. Faith had pushed fear out the door.

Christmas filled our hearts. Joy to the world! The Lord had come into our everyday lives of grief and tears, milkshakes and french fries, a new robe and slippers, punch and cookies, loaves of bread—and the men of God kneeling in prayer to believe that out of all things God does work together for good.

That was last night!

Now I am alone. It is 7 A.M., and Harold is ready for coffee.

I had nothing by mouth—doctor's orders.

What the doctors didn't know was that I had been eating and drinking since 6 A.M. I fed on the manna from God's supply, the Bible, and drank in the promises of God.

In *My Utmost for His Highest*, Oswald Chambers writes, "Faith that is sure of itself is not faith; faith that is sure of God is the only faith."

"O God, forsake me not; until I have shown thy strength unto this generation, and thy power to every one that is to come" (Psalm 71:18).

"Countdown, Margaret," Harold gently calls. "Time to go."

The car is warm. I hold Harold's hand while the car eases into the early dawn en route to New Hanover Memorial Hospital, Wilmington, North Carolina.

1989—and Christmas!

3

Ninth Floor

3

Ninth Floor

*T*he *elevator stopped.* I was led to a pre-operative room where I was weighed, my vital signs were checked, and a few loose hairpins removed. Then came the robe.

Such a wonderful robe, my hospital gown. It was open in the back—and I mean open! The ties were knotted, and my "robe" was worn enough to look like "see-through lace," but not a "Victoria's Secret" special, by any means.

I tried to wrap the gown around me, but it refused to stay. Someone pulled long elastic stockings on me, and I felt helpless in the hands of strangers. How often I had prepared patients for surgery. Now I was a patient.

Familiar faces appeared in my hospital room before I went into surgery. Nurses and doctors I had worked with popped in with kind reassurances. Ralph was there with our pastor Horace and his wife Tennie, and prayer enveloped me like a warm blanket.

In the stark operating room I recognized old faces and met my new friend and surgeon, Dr. Swann.

The day passed into the shadows of night and day. There were tubes, intravenous poles, hot searing pain—then oblivion. A blizzard raged outside, and Wilmington was "on hold" until the storm passed. But I didn't know it. Harold was there, in the adjoining room, and enjoyed meeting people in the cafeteria. He was safe from the storm. Ralph made it through the frozen roads in a Jeep.

Strangers put me up on my feet. "Move, breathe, walk!" they commanded.

All sense of bravado was gone; only a sickening weakness. Waves of doubt swept over me. *What glory is this?* I thought as I struggled around the hospital floor. *What good can come from pain and confusion?* The words, "In Him I live and move and have my being," carried me across the miles as I walked and walked and walked. Never had the phrase, "In my weakness I am strong," made less sense.

The next morning I was startled awake by a team of young doctors. They looked like my grandchildren. What could they know?

They just stared at me.

"What a delightful way to face a new day," I told them. "Five handsome young men to say 'good morning' to Grammy."

They didn't smile!

"We need to think about going home," one doctor said.

"I just got here," I protested.

"Insurance allows only so many days."

"In that case," I crossed my arms, "we'll think about it. I'm running a fever, intake and output seem to be at war. I scream when I get out of bed—and I'll have to go home in a Jeep."

"We can think about that tomorrow."

"Good," I sighed. "Can't even think about today."

"Walk!" the young men instructed as they left.

I held the I.V. pole, and Harold held me. But when it looked like Harold might faint, I straightened up and got him back to his chair and T.V.

"Whew," I gasped as I crawled into bed. "I'm not walking him anymore. He can suffer in the T.V. room."

The soft curtains of night pulled the shades over another day. Blessed sleep!

Another morning dawned, and I was cold. That stupid "robe" had slipped around, and I felt bare all over. My hips ached. Out of the past came the majestic hymn, "How Firm a Foundation."

"But, Lord," I argued, "this bed feels like a board!"

Why couldn't I have noble thoughts? Like a soft, cuddly lamb carried in the arms of the shepherd. "Because, Lord," I pointed out, "I feel like a porcupine. Everything hurts! I feel stuck and pricked."

A familiar chorus kept popping into my head, "The joy of the Lord is your strength." And I had visions of my happy Bible club children singing with gusto, "If you want joy you must jump for it." How I wished I could think of something profound—not little kids jumping for joy.

I wrapped my "robe" around me—the see-through lace one with the knotted ties. The gown was too short, and my knees were cold.

"Time to take the stitches out!" a perky young nurse announced as she made her way into my room.

I looked at the L.P.N. in wonder. When I nursed, the doctors usually took out stitches.

"Whoops! Forgot that one!" the perky young nurse clenched her teeth as she worked. I remembered how carefully a surgeon taught me how to take out stitches. He should have talked with this woman.

"This one doesn't want to give!" the nurse finally admitted after several minutes. "Better get out and walk."

I did!

My white ponytail flopped like a horse's mane. I groaned with each step, but I went round and round. By the time I finished, the "firm foundation" didn't look too bad.

That night, the pain medication caused my dreams to became jumbled and nightmarish. Bits of songs and jumping children floated in and out of my mind as I slept.

"I will make you fishers of men, if you follow Me," children sang.

Oh, no, Lord, not that one. All those children reeling in imaginary fish—and I feel like those hooks are in me.

Somewhere on the backroads of my mind I heard Ethel Waters singing, "His eye is on the sparrow."

Forget the sparrows, Lord. They seem to be doing okay—ate up my grass seed. I need Your eye on me. Look at me—stripped of all dignity, dependent on strangers. Don't You feel a little sorry for me? After all, the sparrows can fly away, and I can't move.

"He remembers my frame." Scripture verses began floating in and out of my dreams. "Dust to dust, ashes to ashes."

Maybe I am going to die, Lord. Oh, well, that's okay. I'm so tired now I'd like to be carried on angel wings—then all the world would be right.

I could imagine what they'd say at my funeral: "I'm glad we all took such good care of our Mama—no regrets. Quietly she went Home—carried on angel wings, like a soft lamb in Jesus' bosom." I could hear my sister Grace singing, "He the pearly gates will open."

Oh, dear Lord, I don't want to go Home like this! My hair is in a long white ponytail. I feel like a porcupine, sticking out all over. My knees are cold. This stupid see-through robe does nothing for this child!

The song, "Am I a soldier of the cross?" came through my dream.

No, not that one. I'm no soldier. Look at me—a wimp! This pillow is hard, and the pillowcase slips off the rubber cover, and the rubber is cold.

Then the children began singing again, "Deep and wide—there's a fountain flowing deep and wide."

It's been years since I taught child evangelism classes. Why can't I think of something great?

"Hi, sweetheart," Harold called to me gently out of the fog. "It's morning. You've been sleeping so peacefully."

"I have?"

"Oh yes, I checked on you—and you've been surrounded by prayer."

"That's good."

"Preachers from other churches stopped by to pray for you."

"They did?"

All those wild dreams: dust to dust, sparrows, fish hooks, porcupines. I decided not to tell Harold—he'd worry about my spirituality. "Harold, you look tired. Go to the cafeteria for breakfast."

"Take a nap, honey. I'll be right back."

"I'll do that."

I fell asleep. This time I saw the beloved pastors praying together, and they held this "porcupine child" in their loving arms.

I slept, quietly.

4

Ma's Home

*T*he *tubes were out.* The see-through "robe" had been discarded. I slipped into a soft, long gown and a fleecy robe. My feet felt warm in fuzzy slippers.

It was Christmas Day!

My son Ralph and his wife Chris came to the hospital with a Christmas candle and a red tablecloth. In a Christmas box was a heart jumper to wear when I got home.

I dipped a sugar cookie in a cup of coffee.

The outside world was encased in ice and snow. Wilmington had come to a screeching halt because of the weather. But Harold was here in an adjoining room, and our car was tucked into the garage that Larry, our friend, had built. Ralph's faithful Jeep brought him and Chris to the hospital.

Distraught eleven-year-old Sarah, their daughter, had burst into tears that Christmas morning. "Why can't I go to see my Grammy? Why does Mother go? She isn't even remotely related to her, and I am her granddaughter!"

I lived on that for a long time.

The day came when the team in white stood in front of me with their pens and charts.

This was discharge day!

I felt like a buck private with a dishonorable discharge—my hair was a mess, I was in my nightgown, and I didn't have a bit of makeup on. Certainly not good advertising for surgery.

"You can go home in your robe," someone whispered sweetly.

"Then I'd like to go out the back door," I said.

"The snow and ice hasn't been cleared yet, so the best place is the front entrance."

"Oh, the front entrance." I rolled my eyes. "How wonderful."

My two generals, Ralph and Harold, went into action.

"I'll take the Jeep and get Dad's car out of the garage. That way we can put everyone in the car, and you won't have to climb into the Jeep," Ralph announced, smiling at me.

Harold took a nap, while I waited for Ralph's return. I waited and waited.

"I had to shovel the driveway," Ralph explained as he whisked into my room several hours later, "and I had the wrong car keys."

Exit Harold and Ralph in the Jeep.

I took a nap. This would be a long day.

When I woke, it had grown darker. But still I waited!

With all this time on my hands, I began to think about leaving the hospital. I had a vision of loveliness going through the main lobby out the front entrance—pink robe and ponytail and looking like death warmed over.

That did it!

I struggled into my red corduroy skirt, a white blouse, and my Norwegian sweater. With determined effort, I put my hair up, but the hairpins wouldn't hold. I tied a scarf around my head.

I struggled with the pantyhose for a while, but gave up. My pink slippers would have to do.

I waited and waited some more!

"We had to stop at the pharmacy," was Harold's apology when he and Ralph finally returned to my room, "but we have the car in front, blocking traffic."

The nice aide wheeled me through the main lobby, past the gift shop and incoming visitors. I kept my head down, but now and then somebody recognized me.

A look of utmost pity crossed their faces. "Poor dear, not long for this world—and just a short time ago she was all dressed in velvet and lace. It won't be long now—a white robe and a harp!"

To top it off, we found a parking ticket on the car in front of the hospital.

"All because of me," I moaned as I got in.

"Never you mind, Margaret," Harold shushed me. "We're leaving."

The lights of my neighborhood across the snow made a fairyland scene.

I was home!

My daughter-in-love Chris prepared a quick steak and mashed potatoes, a pot of tea and a Christmas cookie. The simple pleasures of life come with healing in the midst of pain and confusion.

Chris turned "a firm foundation" into "the feathery beds of ease" while she tucked me into a long flannel gown. I curled up with my down comforter and pillow. Harold sat beside me and stroked my head until I fell asleep.

I would make it!

Sunday came and our seventeen-year-old grandson Shawn came over with dinner for the three of us. His youth and confidence brought renewed hope.

"Grammy, I know you'll make it," he said with a grin. "I really know, deep inside. I know that you will be fine."

During my recuperation, I read and re-read a letter from Chad, number-one grandson.

> My dearest Papa and "Grammy Grubby,"
>
> Here I sit bored and tired and procrastinating on college essays. What better thing to do than check up on my grandparents.
>
> I hope you are feeling better, Grams, because when I come to visit I expect two grandparents in top physical condition. (I wouldn't want to give you a handicap in horseshoes.)
>
> I got my report card yesterday—grades from A to D—so you might call me a well-rounded student.
>
> I love you and will keep praying for you.
>
> > Love,
> > Chad

The "Grammy Grubby" part came because I wear old beat-up polyester shorts in the garden. "These are my grubbies," I had explained to Chad. He went all over the neighborhood announcing, "My Grammy has grub-bies" and the name has stuck.

There is something special about the thoughts and prayers of seventeen-year-old grandsons. I missed my children and grandchildren when they weren't with me. I couldn't wait until they'd be in my home again.

Thinking about them caused the memories to come out on the stage—players from another day...

It was thirty years ago, but I remember each detail on the backroads of my mind, printed on my heart with indelible ink.

He stood in the corridor, outside the door where his wife lay in a coma. His weathered face reflected the sun and wind; his thumbs nervously pulled at his overall straps.

"Proud to meet you," he answered politely when I told him I was his wife's morning nurse. "Cain't run no chicken farm without my woman," his voice choked up.

I assured him that we would all take good care of her. The patient's room was quiet; the intravenous fluid dripped into her veins. The doctor warned us not to move her, due to an obstruction in one of her blood ves-sels. Constant care was needed to monitor medication and vital signs. She was cold and clammy.

One day I was granted permission to lift her up, with the help of four nurses, to put a warm blanket under her.

I talked to her quietly, cared for her, placed warm blankets over the cold body, and quoted the Twenty-Third Psalm.

There was no response.

Her husband came to see her early each morning, then returned home to care for his chickens and twelve children. The eldest daughter, newly married, helped care for the family.

One morning the farmer met me in the hall. "I got a pot of coffee perkin' in the room. Just had to do something. I seen you nurses drink coffee. Just had to do something."

Every morning after that he waited for me. "Coffee ready. Not much I can do, mind you. But had to do something." One morning he brushed a tear with the back of his work-worn hand. "Cain't run no chicken farm without my woman—and all those younguns."

"Don't be afraid," I reassured him. "You'll make it. God will take care of you and your family. People are praying for you."

She never moved.

One day I sat by her bed and quoted Psalm 23 once again.

Suddenly, my patient's eyes opened. "That voice—I know that voice." She faltered. "I heard someone talking. You are the voice!"

"Yes," I answered, with a lump in my throat, "I am the voice."

"I was going through a long dark tunnel," she continued, "then through cold, black water. I was so cold. Someone lifted me and put a warm blanket under me." Her lips trembled. "Then I heard the voice, 'Though I walk through the valley of the shadow of death, I will fear no evil, for thou art with me.' I felt a warm hand pull me back. I heard you!"

Gradually the woman improved until she was able to sit in a chair. Christmas was coming, and her children would be allowed to visit her, two at a time. Her other two nurses and I bought a beautiful pink stole for the occasion.

When Christmas morning came, my farmer was there with the coffee perking.

By the time the children came, their mother was sitting in a chair, her long black hair in braids, with a pink bow for each braid. The soft stole around her shoulders covered a warm flannel robe. She was beautiful!

The farmer gave an approving glance, then joked tenderly, "Now, now, we can't be lettin' you git used to them fancy things."

She understood. Her dark eyes smiled at him.

The children came in two by two. Her dark eyes filled with tears when the two youngest stood silently in awe.

Her married daughter and young husband lingered to report that all was well at home.

"Your daughter is lovely," I said when we were alone. "She seems to have a nice husband."

"He is a good boy—walks soft-like through life."

The day came when we said goodbye to the chicken farmer, his wife, and the coffeepot.

Months later I had a surprise visit. There they stood, the chicken farmer in clean overalls and his gentle wife beside him. She wore a plain cotton dress, flat shoes, and her hair pulled back in a bun.

They stood hand in hand.

"Farm's goin' good, ma'am," the chicken farmer said. "Younguns all in school—right smart too. It's good to have Ma home. Just cain't run no chicken farm without my woman."

Her smile said it all.

The memory went "soft-like" through my mind. That was a long-ago Christmas—and now it was time to take a nap.

This "Ma" was home—and someone would be putting on the coffeepot.

After all, you cain't run no home without Grammy Grubby.

5

Stark White Walls

H *ow quickly plans can change!* But peace is there when we know how safe we are in the hollow of His hand. For me, 1990 would be a year of new challenges. My daughter Jan's organizational skills came into focus as she methodically viewed my heavy schedule. Month by month she cancelled speaking engagements, while at the same time offering replacements. And she gave me the assurance that this would be a year of rest and writing.

1990—Countdown!

The doors opened outwardly and Harold and I walked into a stark white world. It was the end of January, and I was scheduled for radiation therapy—twenty-eight sessions!

The receptionist was pleasant, and papers were filled out. Coffee and cookies were served in a friendly atmosphere.

Interviews, X-rays—then the day of therapy.

"You don't need to stop at the reception desk anymore," I was instructed, "just undress and get into your gown and wait your turn."

I wrapped my flimsy gown around me and shivered. I was cold, so I pulled my Norwegian sweater around me as well. It was warm and familiar—everything else was stark and strange.

My head drooped and I closed my eyes. I didn't want to look at anyone, but when I did I saw several people— all ages, different races, and both genders—sitting in their flimsy gowns, eyes closed, waiting to be called.

I held my Norwegian sweater tighter. Only two short years ago Harold, Jan, and I had selected gifts in Oslo— Norwegian sweaters for the Norskies in the family. Then in Copenhagen we selected Danish sweaters for our great Danes. "We can't afford these sweaters," we had laughed together. "Oh—but it's a once in a lifetime trip, and we won't buy souvenirs—just a lovely sweater for Christmas. That's lasting value."

For a few moments I shut out the present and relived the joy of family reunions in Denmark and Norway. I chuckled at the memory of the Book Fair in Frankfurt, Germany.

Our serious German hosts were in charge of a banquet for the visiting guests. Questions were asked about forthcoming books, and when a German host asked Harold what he did, Harold gave the classic Jensen answer: "I get to sleep with the author."

The German resolve was broken, and laughter erupted across the room. The rest of the evening was hilarious.

One year later we met a Danish publisher in Dallas. When he saw Harold, he burst out laughing. "We still remember that banquet!"

Then there was the train ride to Copenhagen, Stockholm, Oslo! What a sight Jan, Harold, and I were—inexperienced world travelers pulling huge suitcases on wheels that refused to go in the same direction. No wonder backpacks were in vogue.

Jan ordered us to "sit" while she made phone calls, ordered cabs, arranged hotel rooms, and connected us with family and friends.

That was long ago. Now I "sat" with ducks in a row in a stark white room, waiting for my number to be called. I clutched my sweater and recalled how often I had shared the story "Sunsets Never Wait."

Our four-year-old son, Dan, pulled on my apron while I was washing dishes. "Mama, come out on the back porch and watch the sunset."

"In a minute."

Within a few moments he was back, pulling on my apron.

My reply: "In a minute." I kept washing dishes.

One more tug on my apron and his blue eyes looked up at me. "Mama, don't you know sunsets never wait?"

I dried my hands, and we sat on the porch together and watched the sun set in the west.

A molten moment comes in our lives that never comes again. These are moments we hold in our hearts forever. They are moments that sustain us when life is dark.

"Margaret Jensen!" an attendant barked.

I jumped!

"Come this way."

Sad eyes in the waiting room followed me. I looked down, feeling naked and stripped of dignity. Only a few weeks ago I was the speaker at the Hospital Auxiliary banquet at the Hilton. Gloria had made a green silk suit for me. Joy and laughter had filled the banquet room.

I shuffled along without my sweater, clutching my flimsy gown around my naked body.

"Up on the table!" the attendant commanded.

I moaned! Every step in getting on the cold, hard table was an effort. (I had a fleeting vision of hoeing the garden and digging up weeds.)

I lay very still while my feet were taped so I couldn't move. A young man made the adjustments—then I was alone in a world of machinery.

"Fear thou not for I am with you." I remembered the words, but I was afraid. The massive room, the strangers, the huge machinery that rolled over me. Cold fear gripped me, and for a moment I begged God to please take me Home to a safe place.

I lay very still. The room was dark. Quietly I sensed the living Word coming from deep within me. "Oh, Lord, I thank You for the full armor of God—the helmet of salvation, a sound mind—no fear! Let the breastplate of righteousness cover all the good cells. Loins girt about with truth. Let the radiation be a friend in God's hand to search and destroy evil, lurking cells. My feet won't be taped forever, but let my feet walk in the path of obedience. Let the sword of the Spirit rise up—the Word of God. All things are made by You, Lord—skilled surgeons, great inventions, machines in the hands of trained professionals—all in God's all powerful hand. Instead of this flimsy robe, let me know the shield of faith, the name of the Lord, a strong tower."

The Word kept rising up as a shield against the adverse effects of radiation, against the darts of fear and doubt.

Then it was over!

I asked the names of the strangers who operated the huge machines, then autographed a book for them.

When I walked out I held my head high and smiled at my friends in a row. "All God's children got robes," I reminded them as I stopped to autograph a book. (I always kept a supply with me.)

"I talk to the Lord when I'm on that table," someone said.

"So do I," I nodded my head. "And we'll make it."

"Lordy, but it was foggy this morning. Drove from near Clinton, more than forty miles. Skies clear now, not bad driving back." The woman's shiny black face wreathed in pigtails looked up at me.

"Yes, sir," a timid voice added, "only one way to go—that's believing in the Lord. He will see us through."

"You spoke in our church and your *Lena* book saw me through some dark times. Never had a chance to thank you."

Before I knew it, a week had passed. I had met new friends, not just gray faces in flimsy gowns. Faith covered our broken bodies like shining shields.

Harold and Jan were waiting in the waiting room. People were laughing—Harold's fifty-year-old jokes worked!

Countdown! Three sessions down—twenty-five to go! "Let's go to Jacksons for barbecue," I said to Harold and

Jan as we left. It was a forbidden diet, but I felt like celebrating.

Later we headed to the beach and laughed at the sea gulls. I would not allow molten moments to slip away.

Later, I curled up on my favorite sofa in my den and thanked God and my friend Larry, the young builder who made the addition to the house possible! The walls had stretched, and I not only had a den but my own bathroom as well. Happy day!

I fell asleep listening to the Scripture read by Horace Hilton. (Don't tell him I fell asleep.) Later, I would put the tape on again—and stay awake.

Thank You, Lord.

6

Sunday Dinner

I *want to have Sunday dinner,"* I announced soon after I was home from the hospital.

"Oh, Mom," my daughter-in-love Chris protested, "you can't do that."

"Oh, yes, I can. I want, as much as possible, everything to be the same for the grandchildren's sake. Harold will set the table and peel the potatoes, carrots, and onions, and I'll put it all together with a roast. When you come from church, Chris, you can make the salad. Ice cream and cookies for dessert is fine. See? I won't really do anything, but we'll all be together as usual."

Harold was great! He set the table, peeled the vegetables—and the oven did the rest while I fell asleep on the sofa.

As we gathered around the table, Sarah sat beside her Papa (the grandchildren's name for Harold) and Eric sat by me.

I remembered a time when seating was changed. Little Eric folded his arms in disapproval. "Whatever happened to tradition in this family?" he asked. "I always sit next to Grammy." We changed the seating. Tradition must stay.

And so it came to pass that the tradition of Sunday dinner continued. There is a sense of security in order. The jokes, the laughter, the stories from the past brought healing to the places where fear and doubt made wounds.

During the week, our church family brought delicious meals, and Harold and I sat down to enjoy the labor of love. This was a new experience for me, since I had been the "strong one"—always able to give and prepare for others.

Now I was learning to receive, and that was not easy for this "giver." I learned a new humility in weakness—and the ability to receive with a thankful spirit.

Oswald Chambers wrote, "The main thing about Christianity is not the work we do, but the relationship we maintain and the atmosphere produced by that relationship. That is all God asks us to look after, and it is the one thing that is being constantly assailed."

Somewhere else I read that a thankful heart stores mercies to feed faith. Experiences can also strengthen faith. When we have the tests, we can rely on faith that is stored up.

I used these days of weakness to abide, rest in the Lord, stand still, and see the salvation of the Lord.

Since my life had been packed with action, I felt useless when I had to wait, rest, sit, stand, abide. But I learned that the faith of yesterday rekindled faith for today—faith to trust one more day.

I missed going to church, but when I heard the car doors shut I knew "church" had come to me.

One Sunday Eric came in out of sorts. "Grammy, I should never have gotten out of bed. This is the worst day of my life."

Sarah was putting ice in the glasses. Katie put chairs around the table.

I murmured a half-hearted, "That's too bad."

"I mean it! You won't believe what happened."

"Well, what happened?"

"First thing I noticed was that my shirt was backwards, and the tag was in the front."

"Really?"

"That's serious! I looked like a nerd. Then I started to doodle on the bulletin and my pencil slipped under a fat lady. When I tried to get it, she thought I was fresh."

"Oh, how funny!"

"It's not funny!"

"It's not funny." I looked serious.

"That's not all. I spilled the communion wine and broke the glass cup. I ran to the car, just to get away from everybody, and know what?"

"What?"

"I jumped in the car. How was I to know Mama had a coconut pie under a big towel? I sat on the coconut pie!"

"You sat on our dessert?" Now I was awake!

He looked so miserable.

"Well, Eric, believe it or not, I made a chocolate cake."

The horrible day didn't turn out too bad after all.

Eric will probably be telling his grandchildren how he sat on the coconut pie—his favorite dessert.

So it came to pass that Sunday dinner continued—the one constant in our chaos.

7

Stirrings of Faith

My Journal, February 12, 1990

I'm not living well with pain. I'm too weary to ask questions. When I do, the answer is silence. Pain and weakness tear at my faith, and I'm clinging desperately to the Rock. I would probably let go, but His hand holds me.

It is then I remember that I am kept by the power of God—not my strength.

I read that it is best to be quiet in the dark. What wisdom! Our words betray us, for in pain and despair our words come out in babblings and rambling questions. This is the time to listen and be quiet—that in itself is victory.

These days of marking time are difficult. I go from one hour to the next, just staying in limbo, nothing done. Hours that once were filled with joyful, meaningful work, hours that brought a sense of accomplishment, are now numbers on a clock: time for medication, treatment, cup of tea, another nap.

The clock strikes, and it doesn't matter. A basket of mail stares at me. The pen is untouched. The gardens are desolate, calling for my pruning shears. So the days pass.

And yet, a few jonquils lift their yellow heads to say, "Hello." The pear trees are full of blossoms. The iris defy the cold nights and come through the warming earth.

Spring will come! And even in my darkness, the sounds of faith come through the winter of the soul.

I don't *feel* any of this. I just *know* it is so. The jonquils need no help from me to raise their yellow heads into the crisp morning, and so faith rises up to signal God's unfailing promises: "I am with you!"

The machinery of the world rolls on, and the clock strikes again. I am quiet, listening to the stirrings of jonquils, lilies of the valley, and shoots of green iris. Just so, I will listen in the darkness to the stirrings of faith.

My Journal, February 17, 1990

3 A.M. Pain is so excruciating—worse than labor. If I had been given a choice, I would have said with the apostle Paul, "To go is better," and I wouldn't add, "It was needful for me to stay."

God have mercy on the hurting world. Never knew nights and pain could last forever.

My Journal, February 19, 1990

"How was the weekend?" the receptionist at the radiation therapy lab asked.

"The worst in my whole life," I replied, "like being in constant labor."

"After your treatment," she smiled consolingly, "you need to see the doctor."

Moments later I struggled onto the table in one of the treatment rooms. The young man preparing to give me my dosage asked a simple question, "How are you?"

"I don't think I have ever had such pain," I answered truthfully. "It's non-ending."

In a flash he said, "Get off the table! This was going to be the largest dose of radiation you've had, so you must see the doctor before another treatment."

After a quick examination, the radiologist said, "We need to give you a few days rest—then begin slowly and catch up."

I returned to thank the young man—one of God's angels unawares. I believed he rescued me from greater harm.

Later that day Jan showed her beautiful face. Harold had never seen me in such agony and was afraid, so a phone call had brought my daughter flying across the miles.

My Journal, February 23, 1990

Countdown! The last treatment, number twenty-eight!

Jan prepared a party of fruit, cheese, and crackers as a special thank you to the radiation team.

I had made it.

My Journal, February 26, 1990

Jan left for Boston. What a gift of love.

Fatigue is difficult to live with, but day by day I am gaining strength.

In everything give thanks!

8

Chicken Soup

*L*ove came in many ways during the weeks and months of my recuperation—cards, letters, phone calls, flowers, and gifts.

Then came the chicken soup!

When Ralph, our son, was four years old and sick with a cold and fever, he looked up at me. "Am I sick enough for a Coke?"

Those were the days we reserved Coke and ginger ale for sick days. Oh happy day! Sick enough for a Coke!

Now it was decreed that Margaret should have nourishing food, and the word went out! Chicken soup!

Chicken soup arrived in every form imaginable: creamy, broth, even Uncle Jack's specialty.

Uncle Jack, Harold's eighty-two-year-old brother, believed in a "no nonsense chicken soup." His famous recipe consisted of a whole chicken, carrots, onions, potatoes, barley, and parsley.

We put chicken soup in two freezers, and when days came when my appetite was waning—chicken soup! Strength returned! It was the magic cure!

I remembered a long ago time when Mama made chicken and dumplings. She could only afford the bones, but we never missed the chicken. The dumplings were like manna from heaven.

Then there was the time that an elderly minister was a guest in our home and Mama asked, "What would you like to have before going to bed?" Papa and Mama always had coffee, rye bread, and cheese.

"Oyster stew," was the answer.

We opened our eyes wide. We had never seen an oyster.

Mama never blinked an eye—just toasted her home-made bread and cut it in small pieces, then poured hot milk over the bread, and added salt and pepper and butter.

The elderly gentleman relished each bite. "I have never tasted such good oyster stew!" he declared.

Papa chuckled and looked at Mama. Their merry eyes met with understanding.

"God and Mama could do anything," Papa always said.

I remembered Sarah Miller and her chicken and dumplings. During the Depression, Sarah had sold home-made cookies door to door and managed to keep their small home.

Sarah and her husband Bill operated a curtain-stretching business in their basement. Those were the days people had lace curtains, and they had to be washed, starched, and stretched on large frames.

Their home was always open to missionaries. Sarah could set a table on short notice.

"Keep it simple," she told me. "Soup and a sandwich can satisfy hunger—and keep homemade cookies on hand for dessert. People remember the happy atmosphere. The joy of conversation is more important than fancy menus."

The curtain-stretching business belongs to another day—but the chicken soup and hospitality are ageless.

After one of the radiation treatments, I was too tired to eat, but I sipped chicken broth and nibbled on crackers.

Janice went through cookbooks and found a recipe for Wisconsin cheese soup. She marched to the store to get the ingredients, and if my Baptist preacher Papa had been here, I probably would have missed that delicious soup. It was made with beer!

Jan doubled up laughing when Harold wrapped the empty can in a brown bag.

I thought of all the blessings we enjoy and wondered about the people of the world who never had chicken soup.

I thought about Jesus traveling to Bethany on His way to Jerusalem for the last time. He was facing the cross, the loneliness, the sin of the world. One more time he would stop by Mary and Martha's, the home Jesus loved. Martha wasn't complaining anymore; she had learned to serve with joy.

I can almost hear Martha. "Jesus You look tired—a little chicken soup will do You good."

My Jan is calling me now. "Supper is ready—Uncle Jack's chicken soup! Eat!"

I will!

9

The Maternity Jumper

*I*n *the weeks following surgery,* I was directed to "Wear loose, soft clothing!" Everything was sore and out of shape, and it would do no good to have my clothes rubbing in all the wrong places.

Jan marched to the outlet stores and came home with two maternity jumpers—one navy blue and the other a long flannel green and white check. Out of the shopping bag she also pulled warm turtleneck tops—red, green, and white with hearts.

I headed to the doctor's office in low flat shoes, navy maternity jumper, and the turtleneck with hearts.

"Don't pull a Sarah on me," the doctor laughed, "and save those jumpers for my pregnant wife."

Harold's humor and confidence kept us going. "Margaret, I think the church is planning a shower for you."

During those days, I was amazed to discover that while we brace ourselves for the big crises in life, we fall apart at the lesser irritations.

I smugly thought I was immune. After all, I was a woman of faith. I began each day with thanks and praise to God for all the blessings of life. "The joy of the Lord is my strength" was my theme. For seventy-three years I rejoiced in the faithfulness of God, even in hard trials. I knew that nothing was impossible with God. I recalled crisis after crisis when faith soared and we shouted the victory before the battles of life were won.

Now pain and weakness had reduced me to a wimp. I groped around for faith and seemed to have little strength to believe.

Then, without warning, I fell apart! I opened the closet and saw my favorite outfit—a long blue jean skirt and plaid blouse.

I crawled under my comforter and cried into my pillow. That gave all the "what ifs" their moment of glory. They traipsed in, one on top of the other.

Ha, ha! You are stuck with your baggy jumpers. What if you never get to wear your nice clothes again? What if the silk suit Gloria made for you won't fit?

I whimpered and shivered like a kitten.

What if Harold saw you crying now—and all your friends? Where is all that faith? What if you are stuck forever with maternity jumpers?

I pulled the cover over me. I didn't even want God to see me. Who would understand that a blue jean skirt and plaid blouse had finally broken me?

"Get it," Jan had said about the outfit. "Great for shopping and lunch with the girls."

Harold had teased me. "Ride 'em cowboy! Now we need boots!"

"Cool, Grammy," the grandchildren had approved. "Real cool!"

The "what ifs" kept marching in step.

What if the skirt won't fit? What if you were getting proud and needed to be knocked down a peg? What about all those years of aprons, starched uniforms, and polished white shoes?

Under that down comforter I relived another day.

Up at 5:30 A.M.—uniform starched and shoes polished. Home at 3 P.M.—changed into a housedress and apron. The "Sunday go to meeting" wardrobe was limited.

Later in my life, when my book *First We Have Coffee* took off, I was scheduled for travel across the country. And I had no wardrobe!

Jan and Chris hunted sales. I found Gloria Chisholm, a seamstress, in the *Ad-Pak*. Could she sew a navy suit? Jan bought the material and Gloria went to work.

The suit looked like *Vogue*.

"Well, I prayed," I said to Gloria. "I told the Lord we had no time for alterations." We hugged and laughed together.

In a depressed neighborhood, Gloria and her husband John run a laundry, dry cleaning, and dress-making business. Teena, Gloria's assistant, cuts and sews. John comes home after a full-time job to build dressing rooms and cutting boards. As a team, they are role models for what faith in God and hard work can do.

"Now, you need a black silk skirt," Gloria suggested. "Go to Karen's Fabric, get some good material, and we'll go to work."

So it came to pass that Margaret Jensen had a mix-and-match wardrobe for any climate.

As I whimpered under my comforter that dreary day, I remembered how happy I was to put away the starched uniforms and dress in happy colors. How I enjoyed going out to lunch with Jan and Chris or taking the grandchildren on a shopping adventure. How I thanked God every day for the joy of living.

Yet those "what ifs" kept waving navy jumpers at me.

I remembered the time when I was to speak at a retreat in California.

"Oh, Gloria," I panicked. "You know that California crowd! And there is this special speaker. They call her 'Fabulous Florence.' You can hear the trumpets blow when she walks in with designer clothes. I feel like Grandma Moses from the North Carolina mountains."

"Now, now, baby," Gloria soothed, "don't worry none about that 'Fabulous Florence.' Go to Karen, get some silk. Teena will come up with a pattern."

And Gloria and Teena sent me to California coordinated from head to toe in pastel mint green silk—even shoes to match.

"Now, remember," Gloria softly chided, "you and that 'Fabulous Florence' are on the same team, bringing the same message. God uses different people to meet different needs. Nothing wrong with you, baby."

And so the "Fabulous Florence" and the Grammy from North Carolina met. Our hearts were knit as one, and we were both dressed in the garment of praise and the robe of His righteousness. Our message was the same—God's love and His faithfulness.

With that thought, I came out from the down comforter. The garment of praise—that's what I needed to dress in right now.

The "what ifs" slinked away in defeat. The blue jumper looked like a robe. "All God's children got robes!" I proclaimed aloud.

I fell asleep and had a dream. On angels' wings I was in Gloria's dressmaking shop. Teena was holding up a beautiful silk print. "I have just the pattern for you, and we need to get busy for summer."

I was laughing in my dream. God comes to us when we can't find our way to Him—even in a silk print in a dream.

Later that week I put on my navy jumper and flat shoes. What is a mustard seed of faith? It's just enough faith to put on the navy jumper for one more day.

And so I put on the garment of praise—the robe for all God's children.

10

The Bluebirds

*L*ook at this, Margaret!" Harold exclaimed from be-hind his newspaper. "Eight inches of snow in New England, and the news tells of storms in the Midwest. Believe me, our young California friends Zackery and Jennifer are getting a taste of winter in cold Michigan!" He chuckled. "The paper says it will be forty degrees and cloudy here, but will warm up to seventy in a few days. Whew, I'll never forget the snowstorm in December."

Harold kept reading the paper, and I sipped my cup of coffee slowly.

From my cheerful breakfast room I looked out at the dead brown grass and lifeless bushes. We weren't sure how much frost damage there had been to our azaleas, camellias, and gardenias.

The bluebird house looked lonely and forlorn, and I wondered if the bluebirds would ever come.

My weakness was overwhelming, and my steps were slow. I wondered if I'd ever move fast again.

The questions came like darts against my faith. What purpose does this serve? Where is God when it hurts?

On the backroads of my mind I heard a familiar song, "He was there all the time"—but somehow He seemed out of reach for me.

I had known of miracles in the past, and how Jesus had appeared to evil people, even in prison. Why was He so far away now? Why didn't He intervene on my behalf? I was too weak to pray, to read—and I fell asleep listening to tapes.

It seemed that an army of darkness was closing ranks on me, dark and foreboding. Where were the guardian angels?

I slumped on the sofa and wrapped a blanket around me. Fear clutched with icy fingers. My faith boat was going under—and Jesus was asleep.

The doorbell rang and Jan answered the door. She thought I was sleeping peacefully. No one knew about my dark night of the soul.

"I'm sorry this is late," I heard the voice at the door say, "but I have a special gift for Margaret."

"Oh, Billie," Jan told our dear family friend, "you don't know what perfect timing this is. I'm sure it is just the reminder my mother needs."

Billie left and Jan came into the living room. "Look, Mother, a handcarved bluebird."

I looked at the intricate work, the nest and eggs, and from a long ago time I remembered my Norwegian Mama's bluebird story.

"Someday I will make new nightgowns for my girls and embroider a bluebird on them," Mama told us.

"New material?" we girls asked in amazement. "Not feed sacks?"

"Oh, ja, new material, the kind they measure in the store."

"When, Mama?"

"Oh, ja, ja I don't know ven. I just know I vill."

The snows of winter passed, then spring, then summer. Another winter passed.

"Mama, when?"

"Ja, ja I don't know ven. I just know I vill."

Then came the day! Under the Christmas tree four white nightgowns with a bluebird embroidered on each of the yokes.

"Ja, there is one thing we know," Mama wisely said. "Ven winter comes, the wind is cold, the snow piles high and never seems to end. The next thing to come is spring!

Always remember that. Spring comes after the winter, then come the bluebirds of hope, happiness—a promise from God.

"So, ven the winter of the soul comes, remember spring vill come—and the bluebirds—promises from God."

Sometimes we cry, "When? When?"

God's answer is that He knows the "when" and you must believe He will.

My Journal, March 1990

It's almost three months since surgery, and I'm looking out the bay window to watch the sprinkler washing over the flowerbeds. The pink azaleas are in full bloom.

Soon I'll be planting my summer flowers, thankful for life and renewal of strength day by day.

I'm still looking for the bluebirds.

Eric and Harold are working in the garden. I am enjoying watching but long to be out, digging in the dirt. The doves are eating the grass seed; the other birds take turns splashing in the bird bath.

I just saw a flash of blue.

There they are! A pair of bluebirds sitting on the post.

Spring came! Then came the bluebirds.

11

The Battle to Believe

I *need the lawn mowed now!"*

"There's nothing wrong with the lawn, Margaret," Harold replied patiently. "It was mowed a few days ago."

"Oh! It's just that I want everything perfect. I might not be here long," I mumbled to myself.

I raked the leaves, swept the patio, and thought of all that needed to be done—house, garden, even a book to be finished. Time was running out, and I was still so weak. And there was so much to do.

I stopped, sat on the swing, and wondered if anyone could guess my questions, ponderings, and doubts mixed with anger at this restricted lifestyle.

That sweet little nurse at the hospital had said, "Just eat yogurt and buttermilk. It's good for you." Blah, blah, blach! I mentally tuned her out but managed a phoney smile. Inside I was seething. I had never been weak like this, and I knew I was going to die.

"I'll eat what I want," I muttered to myself while sitting on the swing, "strawberries, corn on the cob. After all, I won't be here long."

Harold was happy. He knew the long rest would be good for me. He couldn't guess the turmoil within me.

"We need to start housecleaning, Harold!"

"Margaret, everything has been newly painted, windows washed—nothing needs to be done."

"My office! I need to organize my office and finish the manuscript."

"Don't worry about the office. You just moved into a new office, and I'll get the manuscript in the mail." He paused and looked at me in concern. "Is something wrong? You are so restless."

"No, I'm fine—just fine. I'm just fine!" To myself I said, "I won't be here long. What should I do? Write letters to the family?"

I thought about my Norwegian mama. Perhaps I'll see her soon. Could she see the turmoil in me?

When I saw a few weeds, I pulled them out with a vengeance. The flowerbeds had to be perfect. Couldn't Harold see that the driveway should be swept? No, he was happy watching a ball game. How could he be so happy? Didn't he realize I was going to die?

"Look, Margaret, I fixed a sandwich and a cup of tea. Let's have a party, just the two of us on the swing."

We enjoyed the lunch and just sat watching the squirrels at play and the birds in the birdbath.

"This year will be a time of refreshing, Margaret. Fit into the harness and don't strain at the bit. 'His yoke is easy, and His burden is light.' There will be time for the purposes of God. This is the time for rest." He gave me a gentle hug. "Talk about rest—this is a good time for your nap. Come on, I'll tuck you in."

Weary from all my doubts, I curled up on the sofa and fell asleep.

Later I read, "Spring up, O well; sing ye unto it" (Numbers 21:17), and Madame Guyon's words, "Praise opens fountains in the desert, when murmuring brings judgment; even prayer may fail to reach the fountains of blessing."

I knew that! I believed it! I taught it, and I remembered how Lena, the dear housekeeper and friend I had known from my days as a nurse in a college infirmary, said, "You unclog the channel with praise. Praise is like a detergent that clears out the cobwebs of the mind."

> Forgive me, Lord.
> But I can't see
> Beyond the cloud

That hides Your face
From me.

Yesterday I soared
With eagles' wings
Faith topped mountains
Where the valley
Sings.

Forgive me, Lord.
I plummeted to earth
Passed by the clefts
The hiding place—rest
and girth.

Forgive me, Lord.
But I can't hear
Your voice calling
Through this pounding
Fear.

Yesterday, I was warm
With plans and dreams
A song of praise
Melody of sunbeams
Mountain streams.

Forgive me, Lord.
I don't understand

How faith can mount
But doubt can hide
Your hand.

I only know
Although I cannot see
I will believe
Your everlasting love
Holds me.

MTJ

Madame Guyon also wrote, "God's designs regarding you and His methods of bringing about these designs are infinitely wise."

When I had a busy travel schedule, I used to long for days when I could sit on the swing, watch the squirrels and birds—just cast my cares on Him and enjoy the flower gardens I had planted. Now I had that time of peace and quiet, but I worried about the lawn, the driveway, the weeds, and felt helpless with weakness.

Praise? That's what I was forgetting. Maybe I wasn't going to die. Harold would get the manuscript mailed. He was here to take care of me—a cup of tea, a bowl of soup.

The winter had passed, and the endless radiation treatments were over. Spring was blending into summer, and I would be able to sit in my beach chair and watch the waves roll in. Next year, if I lived, I might be one of the swimmers.

Of course I would live!

My first checkup at three months went fine—until my well-meaning nurse warned me of all the things that could happen and to watch for this, that, and the other.

"Oh, no. She knows something I don't know!" I had to stop my whirling doubts with a deliberate act of the will. I will offer praise!

Praise does not come easily. It is a sacrifice, an act of the will, to acknowledge our sovereign God. Fear, doubt, and discouragement are tools of the enemy, darts to wear us down with despair. Praise marshals an army of thanks to God. Just counting small blessings will bring an anthem of praise. Joy surges from the depth of our spirit and strength returns to the mind and body.

I said out loud, "Okay, Margaret, when I am afraid I will trust and sing praises. I will trust the Lord."

That day the joy of the Lord strengthened this "wimp," and spring turned to summer. Then came the beautiful fall.

It was October 1990—a year since I had traveled. (Jan saw to that.) Jan and I were heading to a retreat where we would be sharing our stories of faith in the "Generation Grasp." Yet I was reluctant to leave my safe place and reach out to the needs of others.

A friend of mine once said, "I feel like a noodle—a wet one." We laughed together. Now I knew what she meant. But knowing Jan was with me toughened up this "noodle."

Looking out over a sea of faces at the retreat, I realized how many across the country had prayed for me and sent messages of encouragement. Now there was a thunderous applause. God had answered their prayers—and I was standing before them, "Looking wonderful," they said.

I was enveloped in an ocean of love. My safe place? I was hidden with Christ, in God. I was safe, reaching out to share what I had learned in the valley, safe in the center of His will.

Joy and thanksgiving surged through my being as I announced the topic of the evening, "The Battle to Believe."

12

"*Important*" *Things*

I *was on the road again!* Strength returned slowly, day by day. Our daughter Jan sent me a picture of the golden goose and wrote, "Save the goose! Don't try to do it all—get the help you need."

Harold was wonderful, and it seemed he couldn't do enough to help me. We enjoyed our molten moments together and treasured the hours with the family. It was good to be alive.

Several of the grandchildren were off on mission trips. And then there were basketball games (featuring my grandsons!) that we seldom missed. The yogurt and buttermilk days had passed, and Harold and I sat on hard bleachers eating hot dogs and pizza.

At one basketball game, I was a reluctant fan, grumbling on the hard bleachers about all the important things I had to do—an unfinished chapter on my desk and piled-up mail to answer. However, I grumbled on the inside and yelled with the best of them on the outside. I watched the players turn around with a grin, "Grandma's here." They knew I yelled for them.

At the close of this homecoming game, the parents were led to the gym floor to be honored by the graduating students. A beaming Shawn escorted his parents, Ralph and Chris, to the floor.

Suddenly we heard, "Margaret and Harold Jensen, come to the gym floor."

A smiling Shawn escorted us to the floor where we were honored as "Most Supportive Grandparents." Harold held his cap, and, feeling very guilty, I held my rose. What were those important things I had been fuming about?

We are not so wise that we can always judge what's "important." So day by day we need to seize the moments and allow God to put them together for good.

Looking back I can remember, with deep feeling, the quiet, nondescript immigrants who spoke poor English in our Chicago neighborhood. When Mama told us children, "There is no five cents for ice cream cones, so don't ask," a Norwegian "Tanta" (aunt) said, "Come, we get ice cream."

Another immigrant gave me a new coat for my graduation gift, and yet another made a blue satin dress for the Christmas program. I was fourteen! Maybe they had more important things to do, but they quietly seized the moment to bring endless joy to a teenager.

Before I was married, several of the older single women put on a mock wedding, baked delicious cakes, and presented me with handmade gifts—one a treasured blue afghan.

Wedding bells didn't ring for them, but they lived in quiet contentment and brought joy to others. They housed missionaries and gave what they had, always ready to serve in the church kitchen to prepare delicacies for the festivities. At the Christmas Fest they dried their hands on their aprons and came out of the kitchen to march around the tree—"Joy to the World, the Lord Is Come."

When I was young, my father took me to packed tent meetings to hear great orators, the evangelists of that day. I don't remember the great orators, but I remember that Papa took me with him on the street car—and I cost five cents extra.

Somehow I've even forgotten Papa's Sunday sermons, but strange how I remember him polishing eight pairs of shoes on Saturday night. When I hear sermons about Jesus washing the disciples' feet, I see eight pairs of polished shoes.

What's "important"? What God puts before you to do—and nothing else.

13

To Believe
Again

*I*t *was October 1991,* and I was on my way to Salem, Oregon, to a retreat called "Oasis." One thousand women were expected, and I would share the stories of humor and faith from my Norwegian immigrant family.

Harold and I came dashing into the airport. The attendant remarked that we were running late.

"I know." Harold slipped the bags in place. "For some reason, Margaret dragged her feet."

"It just so happens," I told the attendant, "that I enjoy my coffee with this handsome man, and I didn't want to leave."

"You are all set," the attendant smiled. "You're in seat 4A."

I like the window seat so I can hide and read.

When Harold hugged me good-bye, he said, "Don't forget God has given you a unique gift of communicating

His love through stories. And don't forget I go with you in spirit and prayer."

I was the last to board and turned to wave. I didn't know it would be the last time he would send me off with a "Harold hug."

At the retreat, the audience resounded with praise to God for my return to the road. Looking out over the sea of faces, I felt their love saturate every part of my being. I wanted to reach out and hug the entire crowd!

Rubena Poole—petite, beautiful, white-haired director—led the retreat. At the close, she stood beside her husband of many years. As the senior pastor, Reverend Poole pronounced the benediction, blessing the women as they returned to their homes.

I watched the Pooles, hand in hand, two precious servants of the Lord, and prayed, "Please, Lord, don't separate them. They belong together."

Once again I was winging my way home—home where the pampas grass blows in the ocean breeze. I had traveled through nine states in the last months and spoken twenty-eight times, but now my plane was landing—home!

Harold was there—always early so he could watch the plane from the sky come to a safe landing.

"This is the last trip for this year," I reminded Harold as we hugged. "Three months home! No schedules, just get ready for Christmas and our children coming home—even the shopping is done, and I've written our Christmas letter."

We laughed like happy children and headed for Dunkin' Donuts and coffee.

October 31, 1991. I heard a cry in the early dawn. "Margaret, help me. I can't breathe."

I held him in my arms—then he was gone. Tall, handsome, in great physical shape and just had a checkup. The oak bowed in the wind—an aneurysm felled him.

"My God, where are You?" I thought I had won the battle to believe, but now I was lunged into another war—to believe again.

Our son, Ralph, the former hippy from the sixties, stood in the early dawn and wept. "Daddy, Daddy, life will never be the same without you." Turning to me he added, "Mama, that doesn't mean life has to be worse. But it won't be the same, ever. Now is the time to give thanks for what we know, not what we see. We know Daddy is Home with the Lord—alive! We see death but we know life."

Jan came—then the family and friends. Once again the family and our church family surrounded us with their love and prayers.

Deep inside I knew all God's children got robes, and there were times to wear a robe of mourning, but not too long. By the act of the will we have to take off the garment of heaviness and put on the garment of praise.

The winter of the soul came, but it also "came to pass." The flowers bloomed in the spring, and the ocean rolled over the white sand. Day by day the battle to believe was won, just one step at a time.

There would be a day in the future when I would return to the Oasis retreat in Oregon. My beautiful Rubena would stand alone at the podium. God called her companion of many years home in 1994. This is the time Rubena will give thanks for what she knows, not what she sees.

Life is forever changed for us—but not for the worse. God is faithful!

My message to the beautiful women of Oregon will be:

To Believe Again

It is that time again when women from all walks of life break away from the cares of this world, sit down by the banks of the river, and find rest for their souls.

We come to Oasis to be refreshed. *Oasis* means that fertile place in the desert, due to the presence of water; a place that offers welcome relief from difficulty and dullness.

This is the place where we are given living water for parched souls, springs of joy for barren places in the heart, cool water to bathe our dry and dusty feet on the demanding road of duty.

This is the time to take down the harps from the willow tree, dry the tears of the past, and sing a new song of hope.

We, in turn, can bring refreshing rain to the dry and dusty places in our culture where weary travelers have lost their way in a desert of unbelief.

Come to the water and dare to believe.

14

The Casserole

My Journal, November 9, 1991

*F*or the first time since Harold died I am alone. Jan and Chris went to Waccamaw Outlet, but I wanted to stay home. For the past few days there have been loving people around me, business matters to attend to, too much hassle—and no time to cry.

Now I can cry!

I see the hoses in the yard and a shadow filters through my mind—Harold rolling up the hoses and putting them in the shed. I miss him. Oh, God, I miss him. It's raining. The sky is crying with me.

I need to get a fall plant for the grave, but I can't bear to think of you, Harold, in the ground and wearing your favorite tie. You looked like you were taking a Sunday nap.

I remember reading a phrase in a book: "What do you do with a leftover life?" What do you do with leftover dreams?

I know what to do with a leftover dinner—just make a casserole with lots of spice and grated cheese on top. Then put it in an attractive basket.

The wind is blowing, and it is turning cold. I should go to the store, but I don't want to go out in the rain. I'll wait for my grandson Eric. "I'll always be here for you, Grammy."

Well, Harold, you are Home, safe—but why do I have to stay? This is the kind of day we'd go to Jackson's Barbecue, then head for Dunkin' Donuts.

These last fifteen years have been special. We shared it all—the writing of books, the travel schedules, and most of all the grandchildren. How they love you—and miss you!

On the backroads of my memory broken dreams return with a haunting refrain—"memories that bless and burn."

I loved you when we began life together with stars in our eyes, dreams in our hearts, and mountains to climb. Then the years took their toll, when your business travel over endless miles left no time for us. I loved you then, when it wasn't easy and the stars turned to tears and the dreams slipped away and there were more valleys than glorious mountaintops.

There were days when winter came and stayed. Your world was your world, and I found a lonely spot for myself. But I loved you then.

When money was gone, I turned my hand to the plow. You seemed to take it for granted...but maybe not. The plow cut the furrows in my heart, and the clods grew hard.

Then came the living water of life—God's Word—and the watered ground grew soft and the seeds came forth: love, forgiveness, and understanding.

Then God took our leftover life and gave us eyes to see, ears to hear, and a heart to listen. We turned as one and made a casserole, blessed with spice, seasoned with laughter, blended with joy and sorrow over broken dreams. Out of the leftover life we stepped into a basket woven with living and learned again how God takes all things and works for the good.

We ran a good race together—fifty-three years—and finished well.

I'm glad I loved you then—and now.

I've had my cry. The rain stopped. The wind has blown a whisper of hope. I will finish the race, fight the fight of faith, for I know in whom I believe. My God is able to complete what He has begun.

I'm on my way to the grocery store. Harris Teeter has sirloin tips for $1.98 today. Fresh green beans, mashed potatoes and chocolate cake for Eric will round out Sunday dinner. Eric can mash the potatoes.

Later that afternoon, Jan and Chris returned from shopping. "Mom, what did you do all day?"

"I cried!"

"Oh, no, you should have gone with us."

"You don't know how much I needed a good cry. That's over! Now let's go to Jackson's for barbecue." I couldn't explain about the casserole of a leftover life.

Sunday dinner came, and Eric mashed the potatoes. Ralph sat in Harold's place at the head of the table, and Sarah sat beside him, just as she sat next to Papa since high chair days.

"How old do I have to be before I sit next to Papa?" I remember Sarah's sister Katie had once asked.

"Never, Katie!" Sarah settled that question.

I looked at my "leftover life" in a basket woven with joy and sorrow, faith and doubt, tears and laughter—all interwoven with God's grace. My sister Joyce sent this lovely thought in a letter: "God's grace is the living power which survives that which would suffocate us."

> Not until each loom is silent
> And the shuttles cease to fly
> Will God unroll the pattern
> And explain the reason why

The dark threads are as needful
In the master's skillful hand
As the threads of gold and silver
In the pattern He has planned.

Madame Guyon, *Streams in the Desert*

It is now 1994. It is good to walk the backroads of memory, to see the rocks we stumbled over, but stood up again.

By God's grace we can finish well.

We will not hide them from their children, showing to the generation to come the praises of the LORD, and His strength, and His wonderful works that He hath done (Psalm 78:4).

15

First Class

*A*re we going first class, Grammy?"
"Of course! Everything we do is first class, Katie."

"Why are we sitting here when some people are sitting up front?" In a moment, Katie was in the aisle asking the stewardess if there was room for us in first class.

I watched the stewardess chuckle, then she gave me a knowing wink.

Believe me, any trip with Katie, my thirteen-year-old granddaughter, is definitely "first class."

A three-hour delay in Pittsburgh gave us an opportunity to tour a first class airport. The beautiful U.S. Air Club, shops, and eating places made the delay a delight.

When we arrived in Seattle, the Nelsons welcomed us into their lovely home. They had become our "family" in the Northwest.

Victoria Nelson, the daughter, took time out to give Katie a tour of malls and special places. With money in her purse, Katie shopped for gifts for the family. This was her day! A trip to the Needle and lunch at the revolving restaurant at the top was a replay of when we took Sarah two years ago.

In Norway, the seventeenth of May—Scandia Day— is like the Fourth of July, and we were going to Ballard, Washington, a Norwegian community, to celebrate. We dressed in traditional dress, and Katie, in a long navy skirt, white blouse, and red vest, looked like a real "Norskie" with her long, corn silk hair. She thought she looked "weird" and longed for jeans and a T-shirt, but when she saw the brilliant colors of Norwegian bunards (dresses) at the festival, she felt right at home.

The streets were blocked off, so people sat on folding chairs to enjoy a concert by the string band. Since I had practiced the Norwegian songs with the Nelsons, I joined the string band on the town square.

I loved it! Sixty-five years ago I played a stringed instrument in Papa's string band in Logan Square. (Papa and Mama must have watched from heaven.) I sang loud, with gusto, all the Norwegian folk songs.

Someone standing next to me gave me a jab in the ribs. "This von is in English."

I kept right in time, and with all the different accents, I'm sure no one could tell. When we sang with deep feeling, "Ja, Ve Elsker Deta Landet" ("Yes, We Love Our Land"), the crowd stood to their feet and joined in. I felt my eyes sting with tears. But I really choked up when the string band burst into, "God Bless America."

Then the marching band was coming, and the parade was on!

I was stopped several times for pictures. People admired my beautiful bunard. I smiled sweetly and said, "Thank you." I didn't have the heart to say that our daughter Jan had found the Scandinavian-looking Susan Bristol skirt and vest on a clearance rack in Boston's Filene's basement. (We shop there often.) My friend, Mary, gave me a European-looking blouse to go with it. That was my bunard.

Two Arab men stopped me and asked what country I represented. When I said, "North Carolina," we enjoyed a good laugh. Then I explained the celebration and the beautiful dresses that represented different parts of Norway. We had another good laugh at my "Filene Basement Bunard"—another robe for God's child.

Katie, with her long blonde hair, posed for pictures as the typical Scandinavian girl. She took it all in stride— first class all the way.

Later that day we celebrated Scandia Day in Gig Harbor at Cottesmore, a convalescent home. The annual event draws out the town and surrounding areas and features special music, various choral groups, folk dancing, crafts, folk art, rosemaling, and a fashion show featuring the hand-embroidered, colorful dress from various parts of Norway.

People line up where the baked goods are sold. To top the list is *lefse*, a thin, flat delicacy, rolled up with butter and sugar. The stories about lefse are endless. One tells how Leif Erickson had a leak in his boat, but lefse fixed it!

A little bit of lefse
Will go a long way
Gives you indigestion most every day.

Katie listened to the stories, charmed by the creative people in their national dress.

To think I had been coming here since 1984. Jan came one year to be the storyteller, and now she has fallen in love with Scandia Day and all the wonderful friends. On our plane trip home, I told Katie how I first came to Seattle after the book *First We Have Coffee* came out.

I had not traveled alone without Harold, and the grandchildren wondered how I would ever manage when "Grammy gets lost in the mall and forgets where she parks."

To their surprise, I made it.

The senior pastor of Tacoma Peoples' Church, Dr. Shackett, and his lovely wife, Betty, met me at the airport. He chuckled when I asked what all his assistants were doing that the pastor of a large church should meet me at the airport.

"I determined that no guest speaker should come to my church without a personal greeting from me," Dr. Shackett replied.

He never knew what that warm gesture meant to me, since I had little experience with airports and hotels. Within a short time I was settled in the beautiful Executive Inn, with flowers and fruit and a lovely note welcoming me: "May the presence of the Lord fill this place." The great sermons can be forgotten but acts of kindness linger a lifetime in the heart.

"Were you really that 'chicken'?" Katie asked as I told the story.

"Yup! I was!"

"Maybe I should travel with you."

"Great idea!" I smiled. "Dr. Shackett's church was beautiful—water fountain, all Scandinavian decor, fashion show, beautiful music—and the men, in red vests, served the smorgasbord luncheon."

"What about the Nelsons?" Katie wanted to know.

"After taking part in the Mother's Day service, I was taken to Dr. Nelson's home where I told stories in his church in Des Moines. They welcomed me like a member of the family, and that is where I have stayed for ten years.

"You were too young to know," I continued telling Katie, "but we were all in a financial struggle then. Your dad had started a new business, "The Master's Touch," and I was working as a nurse.

"When I saw some Seattle T-shirts, I wished I had the money to buy them for you at home. But I couldn't. Suddenly Ruth Nelson said, 'Oh I'd like to buy T-shirts for the children.'"

My granddaughter's eyes grew big. "Katie," I said, "I have traveled many miles and been many places, but I will always remember my first trek across the country and the wonderful people who took this 'chicken' into their hearts."

"What about Gig Harbor?"

"From the Nelsons we went to Gig Harbor to Scandia Day at Cottesmore—and you know all about that—but what you don't know is that a woman named Inez Glass didn't know I had very little money. When I left for the airport, she gave me a large check. I gasped!

" 'That's a mistake,' I protested.

" 'Oh, no, the Lord spoke to me in the night and this is what I have to do.'

"Katie, you must never forget how God uses us *all* to bless people. We don't know the needs, but God does. And then we must obey. I have traveled many miles, in

Canada and throughout the States, but I will always have a special place in my heart for the Seattle area. It was my first trip alone, and I was welcomed with love and warmth."

"They didn't know you were 'chicken'—and broke." Katie smiled. "Wow! I think I should go back with you."

Someday, Katie, maybe someday. And you know we'll go first class!

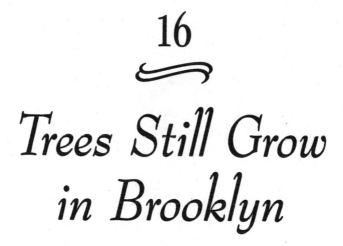

16

Trees Still Grow in Brooklyn

I *had returned to Brooklyn, New York,* to visit my father's church, Papa's place when he was young in the ministry. How things had changed! The crowded streets of Brooklyn teemed with the babbling sound of another cul ture—not only the old world, but the third world.

Papa's church had sheltered the new immigrants of a long ago time. Now those immigrants moved to safer places of quiet streets, flowers, and trees.

Row houses, like children's blocks, stuck together, defending their rights in a changing world. Concrete replaced the shrubs and flowers of another day. Old women meticulously swept the debris off their steps and screamed at the children dodging traffic to play their games, while childhood had room to play.

Too soon it, too, would be gone, and innocence would pass. The concrete of toughened, cynical values would replace the tenderness of a child's soul.

From my high-rise hotel window I watched the dawn slip softly into the morning darkness—as though reluctant to bring into view what the blanket of night had covered.

Yellow cabs inched through the murky morning of a misty rain. A white skyscraper reached into the sky, aloof from the old black, brown, and red buildings huddled together as though to keep from falling down. Boards protected the smoky glass windows. Rooftops below my hotel window were tarry black with pipes and ventilators that popped up like chessmen on a board. Steam and smoke billowed from the pipes.

Vendors carried supplies to the small shops, easing their trucks into the "No Parking" zone; then they were gone again, slipping between the yellow cabs. Buildings rose defiantly, a power play of their own, yet the crumbling store fronts stood—fruit stands, restaurants, and laundry signs.

Then I saw it—one lonely tree in a courtyard surrounded by old buildings. Green with spring, the tree stretched its arms to defy winds and dare the warmth of the new season to come to Brooklyn.

The buildings reaching to the sky were a monument to man's creativity. A lonely tree, in the midst of crumbling brick, was a monument to God's creative power. Deep into the soil the tree had touched the hand of God. In the midst of the garbage, the sound of vendors, children, and old women, a special kind of tree was growing.

Huddled between the rows of brick and stone, a steeple rose with a hand outstretched to God and another hand held out to the rushing world.

A special kind of tree grows in Brooklyn, a tree of righteousness with tap roots reaching into the never-failing source of God's river of grace.

For me, it was a molten moment with a clear message—where sin abounds, God's grace is greater than all our sin.

Papa's church was still standing—another special tree in Brooklyn. The founders are Home; Papa and Mama are Home. The faces in Papa's church are now brown with black shining eyes, and the language is new, but the message is the same.

> For God so loved the world
> That He gave His only begotten Son
> That whosoever believeth in Him
> Shall not perish, but have everlasting life.

Amazing grace! How sweet the sound.
Trees still grow in Brooklyn—trees of righteousness.

17

Hostfest

*M*other," *Jan retrieved a brochure about "Hostfest" from* the wastebasket, "look at this." That began our trek to Minot, North Dakota, that October in 1992, where we were guests in the home of Reverend Paul and Karen Beran.

On the first day of Hostfest, we found our parking space in the state fairgrounds and joined the 66,000 people who attend this Norwegian heritage celebration for four days. We had watched the Norwegians arrive in colorful Scandinavian bunards, waving Norwegian flags when they came into the airport from Norway, to shouts and greetings from friends and relatives.

Music filled the air, while accordion players, in gala dress, marched through the walkways singing and playing their instruments. An atmosphere of joy permeated the state fairgrounds of Minot, North Dakota.

Jan and I set up our book table in the corner of the Book Nook, and in turn met authors of books about Vikings, trolls, and stories of long ago days on the prairies where dreams are made. Our little corner had *First We Have Coffee* and *Papa's Place,* and Jan's book, *The Hungry Heart*, a devotional from the Old Testament.

One cynical browser picked up *The Hungry Heart* and sarcastically asked, "What does this have to do with Scandinavian culture?"

Jan's beautiful smile and a quick answer, "The Carlberg name," brought us a good laugh together. Humor builds bridges.

We met a group of farmers' wives who rendered an impromptu accordion concert, with spectators like us stomping and clapping to the happy folk tunes. Later we sat together for a cup of coffee, and they told how they formed their own accordion band to fill the long cold winter nights with music and dancing.

We chuckled at their conversation.

"Well, my Hans just sold old Bossie."

"Now, Inga, how could you let old Bossie go?"

"Ja, I cried when Hans led her to the truck, but when I thought of milking her at 5 A.M., I dried my tears and decided I could live without her."

"Believe me, I didn't cry when Henry sold our herd. All these years of milking—I just slapped old Bessie on the rump and said 'good-bye' to milking days."

"You are lucky. My Oscar won't part with our milk cows. 'Just like a family,' he says, and calls each one by name. At least I don't have to milk, since he has the new milking machine. He plays music in the barn, and it seems the cows keep time to the music."

Everyone had a good laugh as the stories rolled—then it was time to play the accordions. I looked at the work-worn hands and tanned faces wreathed in smiles and wrinkles. I listened to the music that made the feet dance and heart sing, bringing warmth when the cold winds blow.

While we watched the crowds stream through the walkways, Jan called out, "Oh, oh, Mother, take a look. Here come two Norwegian bachelors right out of Garrison Keillor's Lake Woebegone."

Before us stood two handsome men, about six feet six inches tall, in matching Norwegian sweaters.

"Ve are tvins," they announced happily. "Ve farm in North Dakota. Come, let us show you vot ve bought for the farm house."

We were introduced to an expert in rosemaling (art in vibrant colors), who was touching up a grandfather clock "for the farm."

"Oh, yes," the craftsman told us, "the brothers enjoy art, and this chest is for the farm, also." Before us was a chest of drawers done in the same vibrant colors of red, yellow, and blue.

"Ja," the twins agreed, "it will look good in the farm house."

My matchmaking instincts went into effect, and I decided to look for two beautiful women to grace the farm house with treasures.

The twins came to our book table every day and always had something for us to see—woodcarving, silver jewelry from Norway, folk art—and always time for a cup of coffee and lefse.

All the cares of life had been left behind while happy people tended their booths, where rosemaling, woodcarvers, potters, silver makers, art, music, dancing, and style shows were a way of life.

One young man from California said, "I'm not Norwegian, but I just love these cultural festivals. I come every year."

"Do you eat lute fisk?" I asked him.

"Are you kidding? I stick to hotdogs."

"Me, too." So we settled for coffee.

Lute fisk, a Norwegian fish delicacy, was sold by the ton during those four days—but not one bite from me!

Churches set up booths to serve the favorite Scandinavian dishes. Jan and I had coffee and Jule kakke with Joe, the fairgrounds caretaker, who supplied us with the news of the day.

Since this was a secular fest, Jan and I had the only religious books, and we were amazed at the responses from the visitors who browsed in our corner. "Oh, ja, I saw you on T.V. I'm familiar with all your books."

We met country singers from Norway, with boots, hats, and vests. A favorite song was, "There ought to be a hall of fame for Mama."

Myron Floren of Lawrence Welk fame was a favorite, and he said that the number-one request for the Welk Show was "How Great Thou Art." White Eagle, of Opera fame, stole the hearts of the people when he told how God's amazing grace transformed his life.

It was a great honor to meet Knut Haukelid, the author of *Skis Against the Atom*. He was one of the great heroes of World War II who prevented the Germans from obtaining the heavy water required in the production of atomic weapons. The courage of the Ski Patrol literally changed the course of history.

I had Mr. Haukelid's books autographed for my grandsons, as a reminder of what Winston Churchill said, "Never in the history of the world have so many owed so much to so few."

When people ask where have all the heroes gone, I can tell them I have met one. (During the Olympic winter games in Lillehamer, Norway, Charles Kuralt interviewed Knut Haukelid. Not too long after that I read that the Norwegian hero had died. Books and movies from Telemark, Norway, will remind our children there are heroes still.)

Too soon it was time to pack up our books and leave the state grounds and say good-bye to our many new friends. It was quiet and empty—only Joe was there to lock the gates.

Hostfest had come to a close, and the memories journeyed on the backroads of my mind.

18

Rachael's Song

Jan and I packed our bags into a rented red sports car and headed for Birch Hills, Saskatchewan, Canada.

Flashlights, blankets, candy bars, and canned drinks were placed in the car—"survival gear." We'd been told that "Blizzards can sweep across Canada. One thing to remember—don't leave the car." Believe me, I was ready! You'd never catch me leaving the car or leaving Jan in any kind of weather. I could feel the blizzard coming, but Jan wasn't too worried. After all, New England saw snow. It was North Carolina that shut down at the sight of one snowflake.

It turned out to be the most beautiful Indian summer that October had brought to Canada. We ate the candy bars anyway.

We came to the Canadian border, and in my enthusiasm I told the guard all about Papa pitching a tent in Birch Hills sixty-five years ago. Now we were going to speak in the new church, Lake Park Baptist Church.

"I love Canada!" I proclaimed. "This is my sixth trip this year."

I told him about the farmers driving the tent stakes into the ground, but added that they drove the stakes of their faith into the fabric of their community and fourth generations were following in their footsteps.

I reached into my bag to autograph a book telling all about Papa and the tent stakes. I didn't notice Jan's warning signals and kept right on. *First We Have Coffee* would be a nice gift for my new friend at the border.

The offer of the book was taken as a bribe. The endless stories were not welcome. And I was to be given "work papers."

"Work papers?" I asked in confusion. "I just tell stories." (I guess it was work to listen.) Something was written on my passport, but we left without "work papers."

"Mother!"

Oh, oh—I was in trouble. "Yes, dear."

"Please, let me talk at the border—and no more stories about the tent sixty-five years ago. We are visiting friends. Work papers? I never heard of such a thing. And then you offer a book? You forget we zoomed up in a red sports car. We probably looked like drug dealers!"

Believe me, I won't forget that crossing. When I returned to Alberta, Canada, two years later, I was ushered to "Immigration" after a passport scrutiny. I waited in line with some bearded men who looked like terrorists. I smiled. No one smiled in return. I had been to Canada many times and had never been stopped before.

"Please," I asked an immigration officer, "can't I tell my friends I am here? They'll think I've missed the plane."

A cold stare. "Your turn is coming."

I waited. The man in the front booth looked threatening, and he was giving the bearded men a rough time.

"Dear Lord, what have I done?" I stood beside my bags like a lonely immigrant.

"These your bags?" I was asked when it was my turn.

"Yes, ma'am." (Meekly—no stories about Papa and the tent.)

"Where are you going?"

"Visiting friends."

"There is something written on your passport."

"What is it?"

"You are criminally inadmissible!"

The date for the entry? October 1992—when Jan and I went through the North Dakota border on our way to Birch Hills.

"Wait a minute," the immigration officer looked at me more closely. "Are you a seminar speaker?"

"I write books and tell stories." I wasn't going to get caught in that trap—Papa and tent stakes.

She looked again at the writing on the passport and burst out laughing. "Someone made a mistake and put the wrong markings on your passport. 'Seminar speaker' in our coding could be mistaken for 'criminally inadmissible.' You're a storyteller?"

"Yes, ma'am." Believe me, I wasn't getting caught telling stories or offering books. "Please, can I tell my friends I'm here?"

"Oh, of course. Have a good trip," and I was ushered out of immigration.

My friends were there. "Whatever happened?"

"You'll never believe this—but do I have a story to tell."

When Jan and I reached Birch Hills after that infamous crossing which marked my passport, we were greeted warmly by the congregation of Lake Park Baptist Church. The young people loved the red sports car. We had four wonderful days on the grounds where Papa had pitched the tent—and now a beautiful church blessed the entire community.

Jan was moved upon meeting generations out of the past. Where horses and buggies had filled the parking places of long ago, now young people parked cars in the parking lot.

The message hadn't changed. The Bible was the same. The great hymns of the church mingled with choruses and songs of today. Faith of our fathers had stood the test of time.

At the time, the church and the entire community were mourning the death of Rachael Thompson, the great-granddaughter of the original Thompsons who Papa and I stayed with sixty-five years ago. Rachael was the darling of the Thompson family, full of creativity, music, and beauty. She had been training to be a missionary and had been engaged to a young man who was going to be a doctor. Now her voice had been stilled—silenced by a drunk driver.

Jan and I drove into a grieving community in a red sports car, and from out of the shadows of grief, the joy came again. Joy is of the Spirit, and out of the Spirit the church sang again.

It was Rachael's song of faith that came from the courts of heaven, backed by the angelic choir—a song that found its way into the hearts of broken dreams. The notes soared into lost faith, doubt, and unbelief. The song of faith rose to a crescendo of joy as the people of God sang a new song—Rachael's song of victory. The music echoed through the courts of Heaven to the throne of God. Heaven heard the song of faith.

Jan and I brought the stories of faith. The stories of faith from yesterday rekindle the hope for today. We brought laughter and tears, and faith was renewed for the tomorrows. The joy of the Lord brought a new strength for a people weighed down by the garment of heaviness. It was time to take off the mourning clothes and put on God's robe of praise.

The congregation took the harps down from the willow tree and a garment of praise covered God's people and gave them a new song.

In the long night when darkness steals over the soul, the triumphant song of faith—Rachael's song—will be heard. During the storms of life, when the thunder rolls and the lightning flashes, above the roar of the storm, Rachael's song will be heard. Into lonely days and endless nights the song will come, calling God's people together from every walk of life, through all the toil and tears.

Softly at first the song comes, over mountains and valleys, rivers and forests, fields and cities—God's people singing. A great crescendo rises to a mighty song of praise. The angels stop to listen. The unbelieving world in hushed tones asks, "What do we hear?"

What do we hear? It is the song of the redeemed, the soul set free, the battle-scarred soldiers singing a victory song. The weary, the wounded, the lonely, and the fearful come over fields and valleys, mountains and rivers to sing a new song. The church is singing!

They are singing Rachael's song.

19

Israel:
September 1993

*G*uess what, Jan?" Jan and I kept the economy going with the money we spent on long-distance telephone calls.

"What?"

"I'm going to Israel!"

"You are *what?*"

"I'm going to Israel!"

"When did you decide that?"

"Oh, about five minutes ago. Tennie Hilton called about something else, and I asked when they were leaving for Israel. When she said September 1, I grabbed my calendar and shouted, 'I'm going!' A postponement had made those dates available, and I decided to go—just like that."

Jan was thrilled. "At last you are doing something for yourself."

That wasn't all I did for myself—I kept the phone lines busy calling Jan. We laughed, cried, prayed, and planned the times we could spend together.

"Remember when Daddy used to wave the phone bill in front of you, Mother?"

I remembered!

"Margaret," Harold would say, "would you be interested in seeing how these long distance calls could buy a ticket to Massachusetts?"

"I'm really not interested in details, Harold," I would reply. "Besides, I don't drink, I don't smoke, and I do my own hair!"

"That's when Daddy would burst out laughing and take the phone," Jan recalled. " 'Jan, what can I do with your mother?' and I'd tell him, 'Not much, Daddy.' "

We missed him.

"So, you are going to Israel—start packing."

When Chris was told of my adventure, she suggested that I call Nancy Blakely, a new friend from Connecticut, and invite her. Nancy's response was like mine. "I'm going!"

One day, in discussing the Israel trip at the dinner table, Katie ventured her opinion.

"It's a good thing Grammy will have a private room. She not only snores but talks to Papa in her sleep."

"Oh, come on, Katie. So why do you want to sleep with me and not stay in the guest room?"

"Because I want to hear what you tell Papa."

"So, what do I say?"

"That's the trouble. I fall asleep."

Tennie and Horace Hilton (pastor emeritus of Myrtle Grove Presbyterian Church) had taken tours to Israel for many years. To them the Holy Land was like their second home. Tennie arranged an afternoon tea so we could meet our travel companions and receive instructions and a folder with details for each day's schedule.

Some were from Wilmington: Wayne and Ann Blalock, Bob and Elaine Bland, Bob Caudle, Jane Johnson and her father Louie Woodberry, Jr. Jim and Donna were from Southport; Drs. Paul and Barbara Howard and Billie and Isabel Lawrence joined us from Sanford, North Carolina. Betty Morgan and Nancy and Anna Reid came from Fayetteville. Anna is a beautiful young girl, and I wondered how she would enjoy being with older people. Her response: "Oh, I love it. You all have more fun than my friends." She was a joy to all of us. Janice Wilson came from Burgaw, North Carolina.

We all met in the Atlanta airport, where Nancy Blakely showed up in a striking hat. Since she was a petite woman, we urged her to wear her hats—a different one every day—and we would follow her hat like a flag.

From Atlanta we went to Frankfurt, Germany, Tel Aviv, Joppa, and Jerusalem. Flying into the beautiful city of Jerusalem, a city of white stone that glistened in the moonlight and reflected the rays of the sun, I felt that I was coming home.

We boarded a special tour bus, then headed for the American Colony Hotel, where the Hilton tours had stayed for years.

Everything was too quiet. Double trouble. Horace, with his usual humor, put his head in the door of the bus. "Pray for Tennie. She's about to lose her cool."

Under the new management, the American Colony Hotel had misplaced our reservations and were completely booked. With expert diplomatic negotiations between Jews, Arabs, and Gentiles, we were directed to the fabulous Hyatt Regency. Set on the slopes of Mount Scopus, overlooking the breathtaking vista of the City of Gold, the Hyatt Regency provided the ultimate in comfort and service.

Balconies overlooked the old city, the Mount of Olives, the Judean hills, and the Hebrew University. Tennie had done it again!

Our Arab guide, Jimmy, was the star of the show. His knowledge was incredible—dates, names, history like a tape recorder. His humor kept everyone happy. "Follow Nancy's hat! Now where is Janice—looking at cards again. Okay, Janice, one more minute, then everyone on the bus." Janice taped Jimmy's lectures and Horace's messages.

Looking over Jerusalem I felt as though I had come home—home to roots. We were a part of Abraham, and so was Jimmy, an Arab Christian who believes Jesus is the Messiah.

This is where Abraham walked with God and was called a friend of God. I could almost visualize Moses' march through the Red Sea, the wilderness journey, the Ten Commandments from Mt. Sinai.

Some complain about the commercialism in Jerusalem. That's true, but I felt as though I owed a great debt to the people of long ago who built the man-made shrines of intrinsic beauty as a reminder that this is where our roots are—our Judeo-Christian heritage. This is where Jesus walked. The mountains, valleys, and rivers don't change, and someone cared enough to preserve places for us to remember the heritage of our faith.

I could tune out the tinkling sound of vendors and see the handsome people and the beautiful children and remember—these are the people Jesus mingled with. These are the faces of the multitudes who ate the loaves and the fish. I could almost hear Jesus crying out, "Jerusalem, Jerusalem, I want to gather you to Me, like a mother hen. Forget your trinkets and see the pearl of great price."

Their eyes were dim, the ears couldn't hear, and the hearts were cold. So the trinkets jingled in the market-place.

For ten days, Horace and Tennie, with Jimmy, led us through the shrines of old and new Jerusalem and the area of the Holy Land. We visited fifty-seven places, Horace conducted Bible teaching and prayer, and Jimmy shared thrilling history.

We sat quietly in the garden of Gethsemane where a few of the original two-thousand-year-old olive trees are left. The Romans used the olive trees to burn Jerusalem, and the heat exploded the city of stone.

It was quiet in the garden. I wondered where Jesus prayed—could be under the tree where I was resting. I tried to picture what it could have been like. Maybe Jesus talked to His Father. "Creator of heaven and earth, couldn't You come up with another plan to redeem fallen man? Look at these disciples—the best of the lot—and they are asleep. Are they worth the price? After all, Father, only one leper came back to thank Me. How thankful do You think the multitudes will be? They'll probably shrug their shoulders and walk away—just one more Roman crucifixion."

My thoughts were interrupted. Horace was reading Hebrews 12:2: "Who for the joy that was set before Him endured the cross, despising the shame, and is set down at the right hand of the throne of God."

My thoughts went back to Jesus talking with the Father through long nights. What did they talk about? Was it possible they talked about the joy set before Jesus—even as He set His face toward Jerusalem?

What joy did Jesus see? Could it be that He saw us down through the corridors of time—the lonely, the fearful, the sin-sick, the lepers of the society, the powerful kings and rulers, even our small group beneath the gnarled ancient olive tree who listened to the living Word?

Once again the Word came and pierced us. The cares of the world were forgotten, and now, as one, with tear-filled eyes we relived the time when Jesus said, "Not My will but Thine be done."

The battle was fought and won in that grove of olive trees—while the disciples slept. How many times in the lonely hours, when no one knew, we also fought our battles and surrendered our will—"Thy will be done."

When the disciples finally were awake, Jesus didn't tell them, "You blew it"—which they did—but He said, "Come on. Time to go."

Peter

I should have known
He needed me to watch and pray
But we had traveled far
It had been a long day.

I should have brushed
The Master's dusty gown
When He fell upon His knees
But I turned to lie down.

I should have heard
The anguish of His cry
"Couldn't you watch with Me?"
Sleep had filled my eyes.

I should have wiped
The blood drops—like tears
And stayed awake that night
To comfort through my fears.

I should have loved
Prayed and wept with Him
The molten moment passed
And never came again.

MTJ

20

The Journey Continues

*W*e changed into bathing suits to take a dip in the Dead Sea.

"Don't get the bitter water in your mouth and eyes," Horace and Tennie warned us.

Believe me, I was not about to drink the Dead Sea.

When I couldn't touch bottom I called to Bob Caudle, "Get me out of here. I can't touch bottom." Bob grabbed my hand and pulled until I could stand. I felt secure again, not like I was floating away across the sea.

The Dead Sea lies at the lowest point of the earth's surface, and strange saline formations can be seen. Legend says that during the siege of Jerusalem, 70 A.D., various slaves were condemned to death, put in shackles, and thrown from Mount Moeb into the Dead Sea. The prisoners didn't drown but returned to the surface. This impressed the Romans, and the slaves were freed.

On the North, the Jordan empties into the Sea, but the South has no outlet. The water is ten times more dense than any other body of water. Nothing is alive in the Sea, only rocks and ghostlike formations.

Hemmed in on top of massive rocky outcrops overhanging the Dead Sea looms the fortress of Masada. It looks over an overwhelmingly desolate landscape.

Masada is a symbol, one of the collective memories which has permitted the Hebrew people to maintain national identity above and beyond the thousand frontiers where they have been scattered—a reaffirmation of freedom and dignity.

Our tour group went on a cable car from the plain to this fortress of rock. I can't begin to describe the engineering skills of a long ago time that built towers, cisterns, baths, royal palaces, and endless storage places for food. King Herod had fortified Masada in order to safeguard himself from the Judeans who threatened to rise up and restore the preceding dynasty of Cleopatra.

When the Jewish zealots barricaded themselves in Masada for their last stand against the Romans, they occupied the fort with ample provisions stored in the stone storehouses. Building a ramp, the Romans used a battering ram to open a breach in the rocky fortress. Then they set fire to wooden structures.

The siege on Masada lasted three years. When the Romans finally got to the top, they were met with silence. They found 960 bodies—men, women, and children—in a last embrace. Two women and five children had hidden in an underground passage and were able to tell the speechless Romans about the last hours of the resistance of Masada.

I was told that modern-day Israeli army recruits, during an impressive military ceremony, reaffirm in a ritual phrase, "Masada shall not fall again." Never again would the enemy be allowed to take this ground.

On another day of our journey, we drove past the shepherds' field where the angels announcing the arrival of Jesus were said to have appeared. I saw shepherds living in large tents, tending their sheep, and caves in the mountainous rock that made places of safety for the animals. Children played, women cooked over small fires, and flowing garments and veils kept out the sun and dust. It seemed we were back in Bible times.

I couldn't help but wonder how it must have been on these fields two thousand years ago. What did the shepherds and their families talk about when they sat around their evening fires after the day's work was done?

Perhaps a child—let's call him Michael—asked his father, "Why does the outside world have nothing to do with us, except to buy our wool?"

"Well, my son," his father may have replied, "when you live with sheep, you smell like sheep. But we don't have it so bad. Look, we have each other. The old women rock babies and the old men tell stories. Everyone has something to do. We laugh and sing, dance and play, eat, sleep, dream our dreams, and dry our tears. Now, tell me. What did wise old Zeke teach you today?"

"He was sad today," Michael responded thoughtfully. "He said it had been four hundred years since the prophet Malachi spoke for God. Old Zeke still believes what his grandfather told him—that the prophet Isaiah foretold how a virgin would bring the Messiah. He also said that Bethlehem, though the least, should bring the ruler of the world."

"Bethlehem!" the father scoffed. "Oh, I can't believe what that old man is filling your head with. But I do like the idea of a Ruler to take care of these Romans once and for all. But one thing we know: Nothing will affect us. Life goes on the same for us. Come, we've heard enough, and now we must go to sleep. It will soon be our turn to watch the sheep."

Young Michael rolled up in his blanket, but he couldn't sleep. "Father, did you see the crowds on their way to Bethlehem? I saw a young girl on a donkey, ready to have a baby. I hope they found a place to stay."

"Caesar's decree to tax the world has brought many to Bethlehem. A Ruler we could use."

Suddenly there was a great light, and an angel appeared!

"Father, Father!" little Michael shouted. "Wake up! An angel!"

Glory shone all around them. The shepherds jumped up from their bed rolls in stark terror.

"Don't be afraid," the angel said. "I have good news for you. Right here in Bethlehem a Savior is born, Christ the Lord. You'll find him in a stable, in a manger."

Suddenly there was a host of angels singing, "Glory to God in the highest, and on earth peace and good will toward men."

Then it was dark and quiet.

"Where is everyone, Father?" Michael asked. "Didn't the whole of Bethlehem hear the angels sing? Did we alone hear? Why us? The least of all. We aren't even allowed in the temple!"

Suddenly Old Zeke shouted, "We don't get to go to the temple, but the temple came to us. Praise God! Come let us go and see this thing that has come to pass."

On the way into town, Michael kept thinking about the young girl on the donkey. Then he saw the star over the stable. "Oh, Father, they won't mind us," he said. "We smell just like the stable. If he had been born in a palace, we would never have known."

The shepherds came so quietly into the stable. Then Michael saw her, the girl on the donkey, and she smiled at him.

Old Zeke stood with arms stretched to Heaven. "They wouldn't let us in the temple, but the temple came to us."

I can't help but think that "all God's children got robes." And even though those shepherds would have been in rough wool robes, God could go beyond it all to see the heart—a heart of faith.

21

Snapshots from the Holy Land

*T*he *beautiful blue lake of Galilee* was as calm as glass when we boarded the boat to ride across the lake. As we made our way, Horace told of a time when a sudden wind came through the gorge and whipped the sea into a frenzy.

I couldn't help but wonder what it was like when Jesus and His disciples took their trip across the lake. Jesus just said, "Come on. We're going over to the other side." While He took a nap, a storm came up. Now Jesus hadn't said anything about a storm, just, "We're going over to the other side." It must have been scary—Jesus asleep and the boat about to go under.

"Peace be still!" Jesus commanded. That did it!

Sometimes it is like that with me. I start out on a calm sea, plans all set, and suddenly adversity strikes. Then it seems to me Jesus is asleep and I'm going under.

But Jesus always comes with His "Fear not" and gets the storm out of me before He gets me out of the storm.

I heard a song once about a little boy who was afraid of storms and crawled up into his father's lap and said, "Hold me, hold me, I'm so afraid of the storm."

How many times I have called out, "Oh, Father, hold me. I, too, am afraid of the storms." It is then I hear, "Fear thou not, for I am with thee."

How Jesus must have loved the Sea of Galilee! He spent much time along the shore, talking to people. During the drought in 1985, an ancient boat with wooden joints was discovered. It is believed to be a fisherman's boat dating from the latter part of the first century B.C. to 70 A.D. I like to think it might have been a boat Jesus may have been on ... maybe the very boat from which He calmed the seas!

One evening, I was looking over the white stone rooftops of the ancient city we were in. Building after building glistened in the moonlight. I could imagine David watching Bathsheba. The king was tired, bored, lonely, weary from years of running and hiding in caves, utterly weary from fighting wars.

"Make love, not war" may have originated on that roof. After all, didn't the man after God's own heart deserve a little pleasure for a change?

"Uriah must be a fool not to appreciate you, Bathsheba," he may have whispered in her ear. "He probably never sends you candy or flowers—forgets birthdays, anniversaries. Now, I would send roses every day."

Held within each other's arms, David and Bathsheba were clothed in shimmering robes of moonlight. But God looked beyond—and saw the rags of sin.

Then the dawn came up like thunder!

"Oh, my God," David cried. "I failed You!

"I was just a shepherd in rough wool garments—

"You gave me a royal robe of purple.

"I tended sheep—

"You gave me a nation to tend.

"I held a shepherd's staff—

"You gave me a scepter.

"Oh, my God, don't take away Your Holy Spirit.

"Restore again the joy of Your salvation.

"Against Thee have I sinned.

"Forgive me."

God reached out to David. "Oh, David, come home. You are loved and forgiven. Nothing separates you from God's love. You are forgiven and clothed in robes of My righteousness by the grace of God."

That same love reaches out to us, the same forgiveness, the same grace and cleansing power.

David and Bathsheba will never forget the moonlit night on the rooftops of Israel. And for me, it was a night to remember down the corridors of time.

There are no words to describe the creative art displayed in the temples and shrines of the Holy Land—mosaics of every color, stained glass windows, gold, silver, and precious jewels. They are all a monument to man who used God-given gifts to offer beauty, history, and heritage for the generations to come.

When I look into the heavens—the blue sky, white clouds, stars, sunset and sunrise, moonlit nights—I see a monument to God, creator of heaven and earth.

Cruel, plundering armies came to tear down the temples and burn the cities, but man rebuilt again.

I read that man can tear down the steeples, but he can't pull down the stars.

In Cana of Galilee we sampled the wine—sweet and mild. In my mind I saw people of that long ago time. I could just picture Jesus enjoying the wedding feast, and His Jewish mother looking around for a nice Jewish girl from a good family.

Perhaps Jesus had made a table for the newlyweds in His father's workshop. And Mary would say, "Don't forget to carve Your signature into the table. It could be valuable some day."

Later in the day, Mary could be heard to exclaim, "What? Ran out of wine? Do what my son tells you to do." She smiled. Jesus would come through.

He did!

On our walk on the Emmaus road we stepped over stony paths built by the Romans. Horace gave us a vivid picture of the ancient scene—the disciples walking with Jesus. The stones seemed to echo the words of the disciples, "Didn't our hearts burn within us on the way?"

So did our hearts.

We visited monasteries where dedicated servants of God lived their simple lives. Because of the friendship between the Hiltons and Sister Aldolfino Monti, we were given the unusual honor of spending the night in a monastery on Mt. Tabor, the Mount of Transfiguration. No wonder the disciples didn't want to come down—it was so beautiful.

We couldn't speak the language of the brothers and sisters in the monastery, but love said it all. Leave it to Nancy—she knew enough French to get a cup of tea for me.

The midnight ride of Paul Revere was nothing in comparison to our hair-raising ride down Mt. Tabor the following morning!

Next we found ourselves in Nazareth. In my imagination I tuned out the crowded streets and went back to a long ago time when an angel visited this ordinary town. There were no trumpets to herald his coming. The people in their shops and fields, the mothers cooking dinner and the children at play—all busy with the ordinary duties of the day—didn't know that an angel had came quietly to a young girl and told her she would bring forth Jesus, the Messiah. Out of the heavens had come the powerful angel, Gabriel, with the greatest message the world had ever heard: "God so loves" that He will invade history with a baby's cry.

Mary believed! That is in itself a miracle.

Mary

Luke 1:45—"Blessed is she that believed."

How could she know
When she offered praise,
"My soul doth magnify the Lord
Praise God for His grace,"
When Gabriel spoke the Word,
That this was truly from God?

"He that is mighty
Hath done great things."
Did she remember
When the cross was raised
That this, her child, was
King of Kings?

"Mighty God—I offer praise."
Did she remember,
When she wept in the night,
"Blessed art thou among women"
And Elizabeth's babe
Had leaped at her sight?

When disciples fled in fear,
Did she then know
As she wept alone?
Did the angels show
Visions of His glory?
A rolled stone? Empty tomb?

I think not!

She, too, walked by faith,
Like you and me,
Hopes dashed in grief,
Only faith's eyes to see
The promised Redeemer,
Mighty in Power,

The same living Word
In life's darkest hour.
"My soul doth magnify the Lord"
Though earthly eyes grow dim,
"My spirit rejoices"
For I, too, believe in Him.

Mary's betrothed, Joseph, was devastated. "This beautiful young girl cheating on him?" he cried in disbelief. What could he do?

No one else saw—but the angel came again. And Joseph believed!

Nazareth! The beautiful city with the multitudes from every tribe and nation, walking the streets, shopping for trinkets. Who would believe if an angel came again? Would I?

When I watch Ralph, my son, make beautiful creations out of wood, I often wonder what it was like in Joseph's carpenter shop. Now I've walked the streets of Nazareth, and perhaps it was something like this.

Joseph's Prayer

He held the hammer in one hand,
A rough board in the other,
Lifted pleading eyes to heaven
"Help me to understand.

"How can I teach this child
To hold a nail in place,
When deep within my soul I know
He holds all time and space?

"Please, God, send angels down
To guard this tender child,
My shop is rough with boards and saws,
Wood shavings on the ground.

"His hand, so small, in my rough onc.
Yet, I sense His power
His eyes so willing to learn
So young, yet He seems to tower.

"You said that I should show Him
How to live each day;
To work, to learn, to walk, to play.
My God! Show Thou me the way.

This child in my carpenter's shop,
Is He the Son of God?

The dusty feet, the sweaty brow,
A part of Nazareth's sod.

He handed me the finished wood,
It burned within my touch,
Two pieces of wood—a cross stood;
I bow—oh, God, You gave too much."

22

The Book

*O*n entering the Museum of the Dead Sea Scrolls, I felt as though time stood still. The Book came alive!

For a moment I was back in my breakfast room, drinking coffee with the family and discussing the plans for my trip to Israel.

My granddaughter Sarah folded her arms and made a profound statement, "This family has based its life on the Book." With the authority of a fifteen-year-old she added, "What if the Book is wrong?"

For a moment there was a hush, and I thought of the lives that had been transformed by that Book. The Book had changed Sarah's parents, grandparents, great-grandparents, great-great-grandparents. The Book had been my guide for more than sixty years.

I was only six when I walked down a long aisle in the Winnipeg auditorium while a great man of God, Dr. R.A. Torrey, spoke to children. "I want to give my heart to Jesus," I simply said. I knew God loved me—the Bible told me so—and I knew God had a purpose for my life, and that I would learn that purpose from the Book.

Sarah's question hung in time and place.

Her father, Ralph, answered slowly. "Yes, Sarah, this family's life is based on the Book. And yes, it could be wrong. But in following this Book, don't you think we have a pretty good life? If it is wrong, what did we lose?"

"Yes, you are right," Sarah agreed. "We have a good life. And I guess we have to base our lives on something— might as well be the Book."

Weeks later, I was standing in the Museum of the Book. There was an awesome silence as we moved softly around the many displays. I was reminded of something I read, "The debt we owe to the past we must endeavor to repay by handing down the truth to the future."

The Dead Sea Scrolls came to light about forty years ago and marked an era of stupendous discovery. Following the sensational finds at Qumran in the Judean desert, more manuscripts were discovered. These documents shed light on history, the Hebrew Bible, the Old Testament, the Talmud, ancient languages, and influences that shaped Christianity.

A bedouin found parts of leather rolls in a cave near the Dead Sea. One of the scrolls turned out to be the biblical book of the prophet Isaiah. It was as though the culture of unbelief and cynicism was broken into by God to renew the faith of His people. "God comes to us when we should go to Him," the minister Roy Putnam had said.

Whether it was the old Jewish rabbi looking at the Scrolls through misty eyes, or the young Christian in awe of the clock of time turning back centuries, both could read again:

> All we like sheep have gone astray... and the LORD hath laid on Him the iniquity of us all (Isaiah 53:6).

> Ho, everyone that thirsteth. Come ye to the waters.... Seek ye the LORD while He may be found, call upon Him while He is near (Isaiah 55:1,6).

> Thou wilt keep him in perfect peace, whose mind is stayed on Thee: because he trusteth in Thee. Trust ye in the LORD forever: for in the LORD Jehovah is everlasting strength (Isaiah 26:3,4).

The words from Isaiah that I had memorized as a young child now came to me from the Scrolls. Though I could not read the Hebrew language, I was moved by seeing them. And I marveled at the wisdom of man to translate the markings to make the Book alive today.

For all the shakings on earth, all the daily headlines of disaster, all the changes in our culture of unbelief—still through it all, the Word of God remains. "Hear, oh Israel, there is one God!" God is eternal; forever His Word is settled.

Charles Spurgeon wrote,

> Faith takes its stand upon the lofty rock of God's eternal word, and in all the calmness and certainty of that holy elevation feeds upon the immutable Word of Him who cannot lie.
>
> Faith finds divine certainties and eternal realities in the midst of a scene where reason and faith finds nothing.

Yes, Sarah, I've staked my life on a Book.

23

Coming Home

*T*hroughout the centuries, the Jewish people have cried, "We want to go home." When I saw the Knesset in Jerusalem, Israel's "home" of representatives, I thought of the depth of the Israelis' roots.

Visitors to the Knesset are amazed by a monumental sculpture, the Great Menorah, presented by the British parliament in 1956. For the Jewish people, the Menorah is a symbol of light and aspiration. It has gone with them on their long journeys, lighted through the passage of time as a sign of undying hope and faith.

At the Knesset, I, too, was home. On the walls, tapestries, murals, and mosaics depicted the Bible stories I had grown up with: David with his harp, Moses and the Ten Commandments, the beauty of creation. This I, too, was a part of.

When I saw the painting "The Last Way," I wept. It portrayed a young mother with horror-filled eyes clutching her baby while young children clung to her skirts. A blur of young and old shuffled together in grim silence— a convoy of Jews to be massacred by the Nazis, 1941.

From the East to the West, the North to the South, God's chosen people were coming to the Knesset, coming to their "home." I wanted to reach out my hand and say, "Come. You have one more journey, one more hill to climb—Calvary. Oh, Jerusalem, Jerusalem, come Home!"

At the tomb of the Lord, I thought of Joseph of Arimethea.

> Give me this stranger,
> The One you crucified.
> This Babe of the manger,
> Who was born to die.
>
> The empty traditions,
> Endless laws and scrolls,
> Pious exhibitions,
> The death knell tolls.
>
> For I beheld Truth
> In life and in death.

All God's Children Got Robes

I need no more proof,
I believe what He saith.

I'll take this One
To be laid in my tomb,
This One, God's Son,
In my heart there is room.

Cover Him gently
Anoint Him with myrrh
Outside—the Roman sentry,
Within—God's mighty power.

Give me this stranger.
I receive Him as mine.
This Babe in the manger
Is God's Son, Divine.

As we walked through the beautiful gardens and sat on the stony benches, people moved with hushed awe, sang softly, prayed, heard Bible teaching—and we sensed that long ago, God had invaded the culture of unbelief, turning doubt into belief.

The first to hear the great news from heaven was a woman, Mary. She was the first to hear, "I am alive!" And she believed.

Mary Magdalene

Gardener, please tell me,
Where has He gone?
Without Him, you see,
Life has no song.

Who rolled the stone
Away from this place,
And took the grave clothes
Away from His face?

Couldn't they leave Him
To rest in ease,
This one who alone
Brought me sweet peace.

They took Him away,
My only friend.
Now I can't find Him.
Is this the end?

Mary! One word!
The world burst asunder.
Mary! One word!
Joy with all wonder.

"Mary! Look up!
See My hands and face.

Touch Me not, for I go
To My Father's place."

Master! My Friend!
Have I truly heard?
My risen Redeemer,
My living Lord!

Mary! Mary!
Throughout ages to come
Your name will be known
As the first at the tomb.

P.S. The day has ended. Janice has cards from every stop and messages taped along the way. We followed Nancy's hat and made it to the bus. Jimmy counted heads, and we are on our way to the hotel.

Over Jerusalem the sun sets on the city of white stone. Jerusalem, the golden city—home!

24

Last We Have Coffee

*A*t *the end of our stay,* the American Colony Hotel in Jerusalem graciously invited our group to a stately dinner, fit for a king. (It was their way of making up for the confusion about our reservations earlier!) Dressed for the evening affair, we were all in a joyous mood. The previous unforeseen changes in our plans had worked together for good.

When the gourmet dessert was served, I waited. "I'll save my dessert for coffee." Someone else chimed in, "I'll wait for coffee, too."

There was no coffee!

The Norwegian in me had really blown it. I caused the kitchen to go into a tailspin. Foreign tongues gave orders back and forth while we waited. When the coffee finally came, I realized I was to blame for all the upheaval, since coffee was not included in the menu.

Believe me, I learned my lesson—but at last we did have coffee.

As I toured through the unique American Colony, walked through the peaceful gardens, and viewed the stories and pictures on the wall, once again I was reminded of how much we owe to so few.

The American Colony was founded in 1881 as a religious community, a place of refuge to all ethnic groups, an oasis in the midst of Muslim, Jewish, and Mohammedan slums. But its history goes back even further. It all began with the headlines: "Chicago in Ashes"—October 8, 1871.

Torrents of people were fleeing blazing streets and struggling over flaming bridges to escape to the country. In the running crowds, hundreds of lost children were screaming for their parents. Thieves and looters were ransacking the city. D.L. Moody fled from his new home, built by friends, with only his "Bible and faith."

Horatio and Anna Spofford lived in the suburbs, and their home became a refuge for fleeing victims. Horatio assisted Moody in building a place of worship and shelter. A rough structure was put up, and more than one thousand lost children were housed. The building was kept open night and day to shelter homeless wanderers. Moody himself took up residence in a small classroom. Tremendous revival swept through the worship meetings held in that building. Today the great Moody Church stands in that location.

After the crisis passed, a doctor advised Anna Spofford to take the children to Europe for a rest from the strain of caring for so many refugees. Anna and her children went on board the *Ville du Havne*, which was living up to its reputation as the foremost pleasure ship of the sea. On November 22, 1873, in the Atlantic Ocean, the ship was rammed by a great iron sailing ship. Hysteria mounted and hundreds of passengers fought to reach inadequate lifeboats. Anna and her children were pushed back. The children assured their mother, "Don't be afraid. The sea is God's—He made it."

The ship sank. The power of the Atlantic pulled the baby from Anna's arms—then the other children were gone. A plank floated by, and Anna grabbed on. Finally, the unconscious Anna was pulled to safety by a passing lifeboat.

On the other side of the Atlantic, Horatio Spofford waited for word from the family. When the news came that his children were dead, he walked the floor in anguish. He made a statement that lives down the stretches of time: "I'm glad to trust the Lord when it will cost me something."

Horatio made the long, lonely journey across the Atlantic to be with his wife. On the way, the Captain told

Horatio, "I believe we are near the place where the *Ville du Havre* went down."

From Horatio Spofford's heart of faith came the hymn that has blessed the world:

> When peace like a river attendeth my way
> When sorrows like sea billows roll
> Whatever my lot, Thou hast taught me
> to say
> It is well, it is well with my soul.

Anna and Horatio followed D.L. Moody's advice following the tragedy and plunged into relief work. In 1881, the Spoffords came to the Holy Land. Villagers from Sweden and America joined in the venture to found the American Colony.

And here I am, in 1993, looking at the pictures on the wall of the American Colony and standing in awe of God's children clothed in robes of righteousness, with the shining shield of faith.

These courageous people lived through wars and famines and set up hospitals and orphanages to care for friend or foe. Through the years they have been admired for their unselfish devotion to the inhabitants of the Holy City—to its many races and creeds. For more than one hundred years, the American Colony has been an integral part of the life of Jerusalem.

Like Jesus, these devoted people of faith have walked among them.

One day we will all be Home. When the saints come marching in, I can almost hear Jesus say to the Spoffords and their descendants, "Well done, good and faithful servants."

I am reminded of something Charles Spurgeon wrote:

> The quietude of hearts, by faith in God, is the higher sort of work than natural resolution of manly courage, for it is that gracious operation of God's Holy Spirit upholding a man above nature, and therefore the Lord must have all glory for it.

25

The Red Shoes

*I*srael *continues to be a beautiful memory* in my heart. Upon my arrival home, I slowly unpacked my suitcase, pausing to remember bits and pieces of my trip as I removed each article. Then I came to my dusty red shoes—the shoes that had walked the stony paths of the Holy Land.

"Cool, Grammy!" Katie had exclaimed on our pretrip shopping expedition. "Get the red shoes!"

I did! Not only do all God's children have robes—all God's children got shoes. Emelda Marcos, move over.

Ask Katie! Shoes have become my trademark. My other granddaughter, Sarah, often shows off my shoes and adds, "Ever since Grammy had to wear those horrible, high button shoes, she loves shoes. Look, she has different colors to match outfits."

Now I looked at my dusty red shoes, and my imagination took me over the stony roads of a long ago time.

Our restless culture measures hours and days. The hills of Judea measure time in centuries.

My red shoes walked over Roman roads of stone, the shores of Galilee, the Dead Sea, and down into caves. My red shoes journeyed where Moses had been—in the desert and up the mountain. My red shoes marched with Joshua, and the walls of Jericho came tumbling down. They crawled into a cave where David hid from Saul.

In my heart my red shoes followed Mary and Joseph eighty miles to Bethlehem, then stepped into a stable to kneel with sandaled shepherds in robes of wool.

My red shoes followed the camels with their wisemen in flowing robes of purple and gold. They came one way but left another after meeting the baby King. That's how it is—feet and hearts turn around when they meet Jesus.

My dusty shoes stood near the cross, the pivot upon which all history turns. My red shoes took me to the open tomb, where clothed in robes of glory the risen Christ stood—and called my name.

When I stood with the disciples and watched Jesus leave, I cried. Then the angel said, "Don't cry, Margaret. This same Jesus is coming again. But don't just stand there in your red shoes and watch the sky. Fulfill the purpose God has for your life—until He comes."

I dried my tears!

In my memory I could hear my Norwegian Mama say to me, a ten-year-old standing in out-of-style, horrible, high button shoes, "It is not so important what you have on your feet. It is very important where the feet go."

I looked at my red shoes and remembered a long-ago time when I sang, "I have decided to follow Jesus. No turning back, no turning back."

I never changed my direction.

Now I am home and my suitcase is unpacked and I have cleaned off the red shoes. My calendar tells me that I have miles to go before I sleep, and my feet will travel the dusty roads of duty yet again. I made a promise many years ago that if Jesus goes with me, I'll go anywhere.

Rhonda, my faithful travel agent, is on the phone. "Margaret, your ticket is ready for California."

My red shoes walked the streets of Jerusalem, the golden city. Today I'll walk the North Carolina beach before I pack my suitcase for California.

"I'll go where You want me to go, dear Lord. Just maybe we could go back to Jerusalem?"

26

Take Off

*F*rom *the sixth floor window* of the Airport Marriott Hotel in Long Beach, California, I watched the gentle
flow of water over manmade rock formations. Land-
scaped gardens surrounded the walks; brilliant flowers
looked like paintings in oil.

For a moment I thought about the creativity of the
gardener who had blended colors in rows of beauty. It all
had a plan! It was then and there that I determined that
Eric, my grandson gardener, and I would draw plans before we planted here and there in my yard.

In the beginning, God created the heavens and the
earth—a plan from the heart of God.

Without warning, a long sleek white plane taxied
on the runway below my window and stopped. Another
plane followed, then another and another—all waiting

along the runway for the take-off signal from the control tower.

The signal came, but it was the second plane that went first. The plane gathered speed on the runway, then lifted its nose to the sky and disappeared from view. Within a short time the other planes left, and they, too, went beyond the clouds.

For a moment I thought about death—a mystery. At a given signal, when God's purpose has been fulfilled, does the soul just lift beyond the visible and soar Home? "Absent from the body; present with the Lord."

While I watched the sky where the planes had disappeared from my view, I knew they were there, someplace beyond the clouds.

I pondered the mysteries of life and death, the visible and invisible, the questions that come with no answers. Why would someone weary and bent from the storms of life and longing to "fly away" remain on the runway of life, while a curly-haired child suddenly hears from the control tower and is lifted up into the arms of God?

In God's hall of fame there must be the names of those who dare to believe that faith is the evidence of things not seen. Heaven's celebrities don't make headlines in our culture, but they dare to look to the author and finisher of their faith in the control tower, the Lord Jesus Christ.

When questions have no answers, when hopes are dashed on the runway of life, these giants of the faith dare to believe, to obey, to love and trust. They stand as pillars of strength in a tumbled-down culture and give others the courage to believe that God has a plan, from the beginning of time to the end.

I left my window view to take the elevator to the ballroom where I was the speaker. My theme was "A Nail in a Sure Place" (Isaiah 22:23). I knew that God had fastened each and every one of us as a nail in a sure place—so hang in there!

The following day *I* was on the runway, waiting for take off. It was 11 P.M., the red-eye flight from Los Angeles to Wilmington, North Carolina. Mother's Day with the family took priority over a more convenient flight.

Darkness and quiet engulfed the plane while pillows and blankets were passed out to nodding passengers. I fell asleep with my head on a strange gentleman's shoulder. He didn't seem to mind. We slept, oblivious to the world around us.

As the night moved toward the day, out of the darkness in the early dawn, strands of purple, orange, then a myriad of colors slipped around the rim of blackness. Soon we were engulfed in the dawn's majestic beauty. Reluctantly, the darkness slipped away. Across the sky came the signal of a new day.

In the midnight of the soul, faith slips around the rim of darkness and steals into the heart with a gentle song of hope. God's children have learned to sing songs in the night. Perhaps softly at first, but then in a crescendo of a joyful sound, the song of faith is heard in a discordant world. Blessed are the people who know the joyful sound (Psalm 89).

My plane slipped into Wilmington just in time for my grandson Eric to bring me to church. As we neared the building, the music came through the open door:

> All hail the power of Jesus' name
> Let angels prostrate fall.
> Hail Him who saved us by His grace
> And crown Him Lord of All.

I was home again.

27

The Molten Moment

There is a tide in the affairs of men when taken at the flood leads on to fortune. Omitted—we spend our lives in miseries and shallows.

—Shakespeare

*T*he Gaithers have a song, "We have this moment to have and to hold."

How many times we allow the molten moments to slip away, and they never come again!

During my travels across the country I have heard many stories, and I am now convinced that *everyone* has a story. I encourage the older people to tell their stories so the children can hold these memories in their hearts. These are the moments that will never come again.

I heard of a man who escaped from a concentration camp and eventually, after a tortuous journey, arrived in the United States. He had kept a journal, and one day he ventured to a publisher to read his manuscript. It was turned down.

In a moment of anger, the man threw the journal into the fire. What he didn't know was that there would be a grandson who became an English professor in a university.

"How often I have wished to see my grandfather's journal," the grandson has said. "What a story I could have written!"

A molten moment—gone!

On another of my trips, an elderly man recounted his boyhood days in Germany. Over coffee and home-made coffee cake, I listened with fascination.

"I remember my mama setting the table for supper," the elderly man began. "Then she called us to eat. And Mama was upset!

" 'No, no Papa,' Mama was saying, 'this man is not a good man—no leader of Germany. He controls the mind of the people.'

" 'But Mama,' Papa protested, 'things are better. We have more food and work—and he keeps the young people out of trouble with all the youth organizations.'

" 'So, you say food? Ja, food for the body—but what of the soul? Look at the church, afraid to speak out! So,

Papa, what happened to the young priest who spoke up against the evil? Where is he? Where has Gretta's music teacher gone?'

" 'Ja, you say, "Be quiet. We have food. Our children are safe." So how long safe? When do they come for our Hans? The Jewish doctor at the clinic. Where is he? Papa, we must make plans to escape now!'

"As a young boy," the elderly man continued, "I was terrified. My mother, a godly woman, won and we fled the country. Through a miracle we found ourselves on our way to Canada where a farmer promised to take us into his home.

"It was Christmas Eve, and we were huddled in a corner of the train, on our way to the farm. Unable to speak the language, we huddled together and wept. A woman on the train stood up and went to the other passengers and said, 'There is a frightened family on their way to a farm—penniless and terrified. This is Christmas Eve.'

"As a young boy I watched this beautiful lady come to us. 'Merry Christmas—and here is a gift of love.' We held the Canadian money she had collected from the other passengers in our hands. We understood the language of love in our hearts.

"We grew up on that farm, learned the language, went to school until the day came when I ventured out into the big world. God blessed me with a lovely wife and prospered us in many ways—business, beautiful home, children, and a great church family.

"When Christmas Eve comes, I remember the day hope burst into my heart—that molten moment on a dusty train many years ago."

It was time to leave and my new friends took me to the airport. Soon I was winging my way home.

A layover in Charlotte gave me a chance to visit with other friends. After a pleasant chat and a cup of coffee, I gathered my bags and headed to my gate at the bustling Charlotte airport.

Suddenly, I stopped in my tracks. A call had come over the sound system, "Paging Harold Jensen." I sat down and regained my composure. Of course, there are many "Harold Jensens."

My thoughts went back to October 31, 1991, when God called Harold Jensen—time to board for Home.

For a moment I wondered when I would hear, "Time to board your flight Home, Margaret. Have your boarding pass ready."

My boarding pass? On the backroads of my mind I saw a little six-year-old girl. "I want to give my heart to Jesus." The gift of God's salvation was my boarding pass—not denomination, not a list of great deeds, but a simple childlike faith in God's Son. "For God so loved me."

"Boarding all passengers to Wilmington, North Carolina." I was brought back to reality.

I showed my boarding pass and slipped into 4A. I was on my way home!

Later that night I read one of Harold's quotes: "The measure of a life is not its duration—but its donation."

I turned off the light. The grandfather clock struck midnight. It would soon be another day.

> All the way my Savior leads me.
> What have I to ask beside?

28

The Red Tie

I *went to the cemetery today* to put fresh flowers on the grave. The dogwoods were turning red, and the autumn leaves were falling in the October wind.

After parking the car, I walked the grassy knoll to the Jensen marker. Harold: 1912-1991—"LORD, Thou hast been our dwelling place in all generations" (Psalm 90:1).

It was quiet in the warm sunshine. A stormy wind had swept the flowers away, so I'll call the florist tomorrow for yellow lilies. I placed the purple and white periwinkles on the grave.

Without warning I was engulfed in a robe of that awful lonesome feeling—and cried.

Now I don't cry often, and I agree with the song, "When you're laughing, the world laughs with you. But when you're crying, you cry all alone." And I rather prefer to cry all alone.

Then I found myself talking to Harold.

"Oh, Harold, you've been gone two years. I know you aren't in that grave, but your favorite red tie is there. I have so many questions and few answers. It seems silly to think about a red tie in the ground when you are in a place beyond description—so beautiful.

"Sometimes I wonder why we remember the little things. The other day Chris reminded me that my shoes were scuffed, and I remembered how you took my shoes for repairs and polishing.

"One day I limped into the Azalea gas station on 'empty'—whew! You always kept the car turned in the right direction and full of gasoline.

"I'm glad no one can see me talking to a red tie, but after all, we talked things over for fifty-three years, so it seems natural to tell you what's going on.

"Chris says, 'It's okay, Mom. Dad knows.' Do you?

"There are always some things I wish you didn't see, but knowing you—you saw!

"The other day I came to church and Katie discovered I had two different earrings—one white and one bright blue. And that's not all. Another Sunday during prayer, Katie discovered that my shower cap was entwined in my belt. I'll never know how that happened, but during the time when every head was bowed and every eye closed (hopefully!), Katie untangled my shower cap. Shows how much she prays!

"Of course, Katie thought it was hysterical. Chris didn't think it was funny. 'Mom, don't be in such a hurry.' Sounds like you!

"Last Saturday I left my purse in the shopping cart in the Harris Teeter parking lot. Needless to say I was frantic when I missed the purse and headed back to the grocery store, praying all the way that a guardian angel would take care of my purse. Well, he did!

"Richard, a carry out boy, found the purse in the parking lot and believe me, I hugged that 'angel' and thanked him. Did you know about that?

"By the way, we had a birthday party for Uncle Jack—eighty-seven years old.

"Well, here I am sounding like a six o'clock news reporter, giving you a blow-by-blow account of the family. Ridiculous, I know, when you have a box seat in the arena of heavenly witnesses. Do you?

"Jan is the beloved first lady of Gordon College, and she has your sensitive heart and listening ear. Her warmth and humor make a good companion to her husband Jud's presidential authority.

"When I wear the beautiful pearls you gave me years ago, I thank you that you, the romantic, gave pearls instead of the vacuum cleaner this practical Norwegian wanted. Vacuum cleaners have come and gone. The pearls remain a beautiful memory and a prized possession.

"Jan, who has your grey Oldsmobile, talks to you in the car. She thinks she can smell your Aqua Velva and knows you are near. Are you?

"Ralph misses you, especially the little things—playing games, shopping for material at Lowe's, meeting at coffee shops where you talked over plans. You should see Dutch Square. It's almost filled up, and you were right—a good place to build his shop, 'The Master's Touch.'

"Ralph is like you in many ways. He has the same humor, only his jokes are new. But even when he tells your fifty-year-old jokes, we all laugh.

"We have our tears, but most of the time we laugh at the happy memories. Ralph sits in your place at the table and Sarah sits beside him, just as she did when she sat beside you in her high chair. To you, she was Sarah, the princess.

"By the way, Sarah is Hoggard's track star, and she got her driver's license. We pray a lot! If you have any clout in Heaven, how about some extra guardian angels?

"Katie thinks school is for making friends—until she got stuck with her mother for a teacher. Now she studies!

"One day cousin Paulie was up to mischief, and big brother Benjamin said, 'Cool it, Paulie. Uncle Papa is watching.' Paulie cooled it! Were you watching?

"When we sing 'Amazing Grace' in church I smile inwardly, remembering how you looked so pious when you

sang the part "that saved a wretch like you" and gave me
a nudge.

"All the grandchildren want something that belongs
to you. Can you believe it—Heather, heading for medical school, wears your old paint shirt? Sarah and Katie
have your T-shirts. Gloria cried when Shawn asked her
to alter one of your suits. 'Papa and I understood each
other,' was all he said. Chad won't part with your boots.
Eric has your jewelry case and chest of drawers. Ralph
has your turquoise ring—the gift from Jan.

"When Shawn and Chad had their twenty-first birthdays, I gave them two of your marked Bibles, with some
of your notes. In a small heart box, beside your picture,
I have your wedding ring. I also have the small Bible you
used to keep in your coat pocket.

"Dan and Virginia are still in California.

"Remember when you made the sign and hung it on
the clothesline: THE SISTERS ARE COMING! HELP!
Well, they keep coming!

"My sister Jeanelle and her husband Peter moved
back to Wilmington. Remember how you said no one was
good enough for my youngest sister, Jeanelle, and no one
was good enough for our friend Peter? So we took care
of that and brought them together. Hurrah for our team!

"Doris is blessed to have all her family near by. What
a beautiful place Doris and Dave have for their family
reunions.

"Grace keeps us all in touch with each other—our special sister.

"I'm going to Joyce and Howard's in Arkansas for Thanksgiving. Howard is just like you. He tells the same jokes, and we still laugh. Howard knows how to prepare a turkey on the grill—the best ever! I'll be working on my Christmas letter. Joyce will help her 'old' sister to address more than four hundred envelopes! Whew!

"It must have been some reunion when my brother Gordon welcomed his precious Alice. Wish you could tell us about that.

"The children were concerned about me living alone. I'm ashamed to admit how long it took me to work in the office out back after you went Home. I kept bringing my work into the house. One day Ralph had a great surprise for me—a beautiful black Doberman, much like the one we had when Ralph was small.

"I've named her Scout. She stays beside the office door or sits beside me with her head in my lap. I even understand dog talk. What a gift she is! Now I can write in my office for hours. The back yard is fenced in so she can chase squirrels all day.

"Sometimes I wonder how much you know. Do you miss us? Horace Hilton says we are all close, hid with Christ in God, and a thin veil hides the seeing from believing.

"I often wonder if you are aware of how fast our culture is slipping away from our Christian-Judeo roots. There are no absolutes taught to this generation. There seems to be increasing hostility to our faith.

"When I read the Scriptures and listen to Bible teachers, I wonder how long before the midnight hour. Jesus said He would come again and I wonder how soon that could be. Sometimes I wonder how much you know.

"Did you see Ralph when he served communion Sunday? This was the boy we prayed for, and he came home to God and to us. Now he is an elder in Myrtle Grove Presbyterian Church. He is loved and respected. You'd be so proud—then again I guess you know all that.

"When I see my name on the marker, Margaret Tweeten, 1916-___, I wonder how much time I have. Well, I've come too far to turn back, and my prayer is that all the family will be together someday. 'Even so, come, Lord Jesus.'

"In the meantime we do our best to fulfill the purpose God has for each one of us.

"The flower beds are beautiful, and Buddy comes tomorrow to trim the red tip bushes you planted. He keeps the lawn mowed—just like you like it.

"Wow! I have to leave! I just stepped into an ant hill and those fire ants are in my shoes, and I'm dancing all around this grave. What a sight! Glad no one is around here.

"Now the mosquitoes are eating me alive. Sorry—no time for tears or sentiment now. I'll talk to you later. Next time I'll bring Raid.

"But I won't stay long next time, just long enough to bring the yellow lilies. Besides, it is ridiculous to talk to a red tie when I know you aren't in that grave.

"You probably know everything I've been telling you, but anyhow, it helped me to talk where no one can see me.

"I'll be careful about the earrings and will bring my shoes to the repair shop.

"In the meantime, I'll just walk by faith. Someday I'll understand."

Later that evening, I picked up one of Harold's old books (from the 1800s) and read his markings: "There were communications between the cross of Calvary and the throne of God which lay far beyond the highest range of created intelligence" (C.H. Mackintosh).

Faith slipped around the rim of darkness and hope pointed to a time beyond our understanding.

I turned off the light and fell asleep, secure in God's love.

29

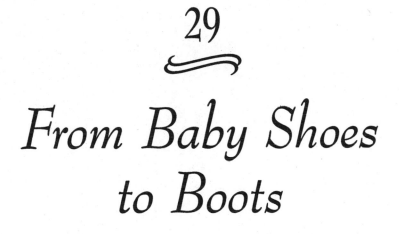

From Baby Shoes to Boots

*M*y plane slipped over a city of lights and eased into the Calgary airport. New friends met me upon my arrival, and we were on the road again, this time to Lake Louise, Alberta. Darkness kept the magnificent view that I had read about hidden from sight as we wound up steep mountain trails.

About 2 A.M. (my time) I was settled in a beautiful room on the top floor of the most luxurious hotel, Chateau Lake Louise. Under a down comforter I forgot all about the scenery and drifted into a deep sleep. It had been a long day.

When the morning sun filtered through the partially closed drapes, I opened the window and gazed in awesome wonder at the magnificent view before me. The blue lake, with layers of ice crackling in the morning sun, made a sound like chimes in the wind. Across the turquoise lake, colored by the melting glacier silt, rose the majestic Mount Victoria and Victoria glacier, both named for the queen. The lake itself was named for Princess Louise Caroline Alberta, the daughter of Queen Victoria.

Into this beautiful setting the women of Canada were coming to a conference. Not only would they gather to enjoy the awesome beauty of creation, but they were coming to worship the Creator, clothed in power and majesty.

When the conference was over I found myself on the road again, traveling through mountains, then the open prairie of cattle land—cowboy country.

A huge boot rising to the sky advertised the factory where genuine cowboy boots were made. It reminded me of something my grandson Shawn had once said, "Grammy, my faith began in baby shoes. Now my faith walks in boots."

Baby shoes? That's how we begin—soft, hand-knit booties. Then we move on to the sturdy Buster Brown shoes. Then it's row upon row of shoes—running, basketball, walking, soccer, boots, pumps, sandals—on and on. All God's children got shoes.

In looking back over the roads I have traveled, my shoes have taken me through endless airports, from Maine to Florida, from Boston to Los Angeles, the Midwest, the South, and now through Canadian mountains and an endless prairie.

Across the backroads of my mind I see the faces of mothers, daughters, sisters, aunts, grandmothers, and friends coming from the East and West, the North and South, to attend retreats, seminars, conferences with a hunger to hear from God.

From the dusty roads of demanding duty they come to bathe their weary feet in cool water by the river of life. In spite of broken dreams, broken promises, and broken hearts they come.

Some come in baby shoes to take that first step of faith, like a child, and open their heart to the Savior's love. Others have journeyed over rough roads and their shoes are beaten and worn. They long to turn back but deep within the innermost being there is the knowledge that "I can do all things through Christ who strengthens me."

The roads of life demand shoes of iron. The way is often rough, the trail winding, and the mountain climb steep. Yet, they still keep coming. Baby shoes then boots have weathered the long journey.

They also come in robes—all God's children got robes. There are soft shawls for the very young, while others wear robes of sorrow and grief. Some come robed in shells of bitterness—too hurt to trust again. But they come—the young, the old, the believing, and the doubting. "There has to be more to life" echoes in their hearts.

There is!

Softly, like an evening sunset, the stories of faith, love, humor blended with God's living Word slip through the defenses and God's love comes through. When that happens, the baby-shoe faith, so small, so fragile, takes that first step into God's love. Then faith comes one step at a time, until I can hear the march of "faith boots"— boots to stand, to walk, to run, to leap. The boots march over the stony roads of life, climb the highest mountain, stumble through the valley of sorrow, but they come, one step at a time.

And our worn-out robes—like a burst of sunrise in all its golden splendor, God brings out *His* robes of righteousness. We are clothed in His salvation, and we put on the garments of praise. Then the robes of power and strength cover God's children.

The old robes are gone! All God's children got robes of glory.

From our first baby shoes, from the tattered rags of yesterday, we put on our faith boots and the garments of salvation and walk with God.

Wear your robe with flair!

Let Me Get Home Before Dark

It's sundown, Lord.
The shadows of my life stretch back
   into the dimness of the
   years long spent.
I fear not death, for the grim betrays
   himself at last,
   thrusting me forever into life:
Life with you, unsoiled and free.
But I do fear.
I fear that dark spectre
   may come too soon—
   or do I mean, too late?
That I should end before I finish or
   finish, but not well.
That I should stain your honor,
   shame your name,
   grieve your loving heart.
Few, they tell me, finish well...
Lord, let me get home before dark.
The darkness of a spirit
   grown mean and small, fruit shriveled
   on the vine,
   bitter to the taste of my companions,
   burden to be borne by those
   brave few who love me still.

No, Lord. Let the fruit grow
   lush and sweet,
    A joy to all who taste;
Spirit-sign of God at work,
    stronger, fuller, brighter at the end.
Lord, let me get home before dark.
The darkness of tattered gifts,
    rust-locked, half-spent or ill-spent,
A life that once was used of God
    now set aside.
Grief for glories gone or
Fretting for a task God never gave.
Mourning in the hollow chambers of memory,
Gazing on the faded banners of
    victories long gone.
Cannot I run well unto the end?
Lord, let me get home before dark.
The outer me decays—
    I do not fret or ask reprieve.
The ebbing strength but weans me
    from mother earth
      and grows me up for heaven.
I do not cling to shadows cast by immortality.
I do not patch the scaffold lent
    to build the real, eternal me.

All God's Children Got Robes

I do not clutch about me my cocoon,
   vainly struggling to hold hostage
   A free spirit pressing to be born.
But will I reach the gate
   in lingering pain, body distorted,
   grotesque?
Or will it be a mind
   wandering untethered among
   light phantasies or
   grim terrors?
Of your grace, Father, I humbly ask...
Let me get home before dark.

Robertson McQuilkin
(Inspired by a message from Dr. Havner)
1981